A Lewin

Information Management

The Chartered Institute of Management Accountants

CIMA

First published in 1998 by:
The Chartered Institute of Management Accountants
63 Portland Place
London
W1N 4AB

ISBN 1 874784 74 4

The publishers of this book consider that it is a worthwhile contribution to discussion, without necessarily sharing the views expressed, which are those of the authors.

No responsibility for loss occasioned to any person acting or refraining from action as a result of any material in this publication can be accepted by the authors or publishers.

Information Management

Contents

CONTENTS

Information Management

Introduction

The aim of this book is to provide an introduction to the field of information management. This is achieved by a series of commentaries and readings in the subject, the latter being drawn from a wide range of sources. This provides the reader with an introduction to some of the main areas of information management followed by concise theoretical and practical applications of that area.

The book is divided into four main sections:

1. *Information resource management*
   This section investigates the information requirements of different management levels and the form of the information that should be provided for these different levels.
2. *Information systems*
   Information has to be provided by some form of system, which will normally be computerised. This section provides a closer look at how those systems are established, and investigates how an organisation can ensure that the information system actually supports its business objectives.
3. *Management information systems*
   A MIS is one of the more important methods of providing information to different management levels. This section investigates some of the different types of MIS available, and the format of the information that each provides. The section concludes with an examination of the Internet and intranets and their use within an organisation.
4. *Information and employment*
   The final section investigates the effect of changing information and information systems on the work patterns and practices of organisations and individuals. This section is designed as a reminder that it is easy to look at the management of information, but forget the effect of new information structures on the people using them.

Each article commences with an introduction by the author. The commentary is meant to provide some food for thought prior to reading the article and, in some situations, provide some of the background theory of information management to which the article refers.

Sections can be read in any order, so please pick and choose the areas that you are interested in. I hope that you find the information contained in this publication useful and a source of ideas for the use of information in your organisation.

A Lewin

Chapter 1

Information Resource Management

1.1 INTRODUCTION

Information resource management relates to the information that is required by organisations and individuals, and how that information is accumulated and used.

The articles in this section are:

- 'Can't live without IT' – a small diversion to see how much you really know about the use of information technology.
- 'Lateral benchmarking' – how information from different external sources can be used in benchmarking exercises.
- 'Information for strategic management' – investigates what information users actually need and where this information comes from.
- 'Does the spend justify the means?' – looks at the problem of measuring the benefits of new information systems.
- 'A source of competitive advantage' – provides an introduction to the problem of checking that information systems are, in fact, providing competitive advantage for the organisation.

1.2 HOW GOOD IS YOUR KNOWLEDGE OF IT?

It is always tempting to think that you, or your organisation, are falling behind in the use of technology, or are not using the latest version of a computer program. In some situations, this fear will be justified, although in many others it will not be. Almost all management accountants will use a computer and so will have access to their organisation's accounting data from their desk. However, use of other computer applications such as EISs is still more limited than literature or even examination questions would lead you to believe.

This article is based on a survey of 1,300 management accountants carried out in 1994 by the Tate Bramald Consultancy. Although the results are now a few years out of date, almost all the conclusions still appear to be valid. As a challenge, why not answer the nine questions below and then read the survey results? You may be surprised to find that your and your organisation's use of IT is not as out of date as you expected.

Question	Your response
1. How many management accountants actually use a computer (as a percentage of the total)?	
2. What are the most important application packages for a management accountant?	
3. How many management accountants use an executive information system more than any other type of package?	
4. Why do many companies not make accounting information available to other departments?	
5. How many respondents to the questionnaire thought IT benefits were significant (as a percentage)?	
6. What restricts people from using IT in companies?	
7. Which type of packages scored well in terms of reliability and ease of use?	
8. What benefit of using IT is most important to management accountants?	
9. As a percentage, how many management accountants do not see any benefit from using IT?	

CAN'T LIVE WITHOUT IT
Yvette Page, *Softworld Magazine*, 12 January 1995

A few years ago the mere mention of the words 'information technology' would be sufficient to trigger a riot in many organisations. To all but computer buffs, the suggestion to an employee that a PC should be installed on his or her desk would get the same reaction as a request to ride the space shuttle to the moon.

But companies were not deterred. After much perseverance and investment, most have persuaded their employees to change their attitudes towards IT.

Question the same employees today and they will probably say that their workstations are almost collapsing under the weight of state-of-the-art technology.

However, an accurate picture of the situation is harder to define. A survey of management accountants on their use of IT, conducted by the Tate Bramald Consultancy recently, clarified the situation to some extent. The survey's respondents, 1,300 members of the Chartered Institute of Management Accountants, found that not all companies are as forward thinking as they would have us believe, while others will always be ahead of the game.

More than 99 per cent of respondents used computers in their organisation and almost all had at least one computer within the finance department. Around 50 per cent of the sample purchase software directly from the developer, with less than 33 per cent buying from a dealer and just 4 per cent using a retailer. The role of mail order was found to be insignificant.

For management accountants, spreadsheets proved to be the most widely used application (see Figure 1). Lotus 1-2-3 was found to be the most popular spreadsheet package, followed by Microsoft Excel and Supercalc. The two biggest packages, Lotus and Microsoft, accounted for 83 per cent of the packages used by respondents. Accounting packages were found to be used by almost 30.5 per cent of those who responded to the survey; the use of word processing and database packages fell a long way behind.

Executive information systems, or as they are now more often called, 'enterprise' or even 'everyone's' information systems, were found to be used less widely. Only 2 per cent of respondents said it was the application they used most in their work, while just 35 per cent claimed to have any contact with an EIS system.

Figure 1: Which of the following applications do you use in your work?

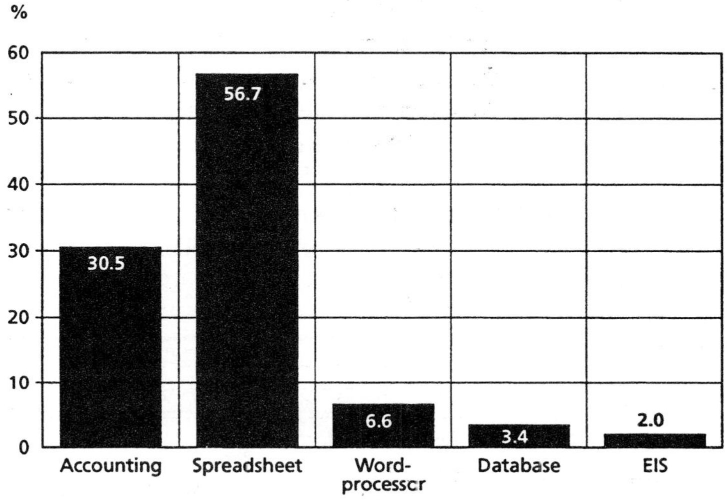

Not only accountants lack open access to information. Departments outside finance were shown to have on-line access to accounting information in fewer than 50 per cent of the companies questioned (see Figure 2), although the figure was larger in those with more than 250 employees. In more than 58 per cent of smaller companies, other departments did not have access to accounting information.

Figure 2: Do other departments, outside finance, have on-line access to accounting data?

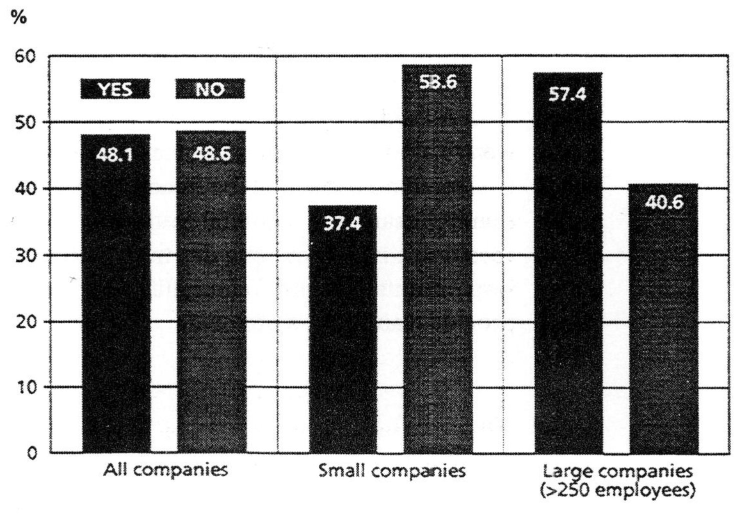

Of course, for some companies, making such information available is technically difficult, but it is alarming that in 75 per cent of the small companies and 60 per cent of the large companies in which accounting information was not available to other departments, it was claimed that the company would not want the information to be available, even if technology allowed it to be.

Individual companies gave their own reasons for their decisions on this subject. Some maintained that such information was not relevant to the jobs of employees in other departments, while others saw the availability of such information to be divisive as regards internal company politics. Many still held the view that information is power: failure to devolve information was often cited as the preference of the management.

While not everyone in an organisation was able to benefit from shared information, the survey showed that the advantages of information technology are now widely recognised. Around 40 per cent of respondents to the survey said they found the benefits from IT to be significant (see Figure 3). However, it is also accepted within most organisations that the benefits of technology could be increased. More than 50 per cent of those questioned said that their company's use of IT could be improved. This was often the case in many of the large companies.

Figure 3: Considering the overall role IT plays in your organisation's management accountancy/reporting, which of the following statements do you most agree with?

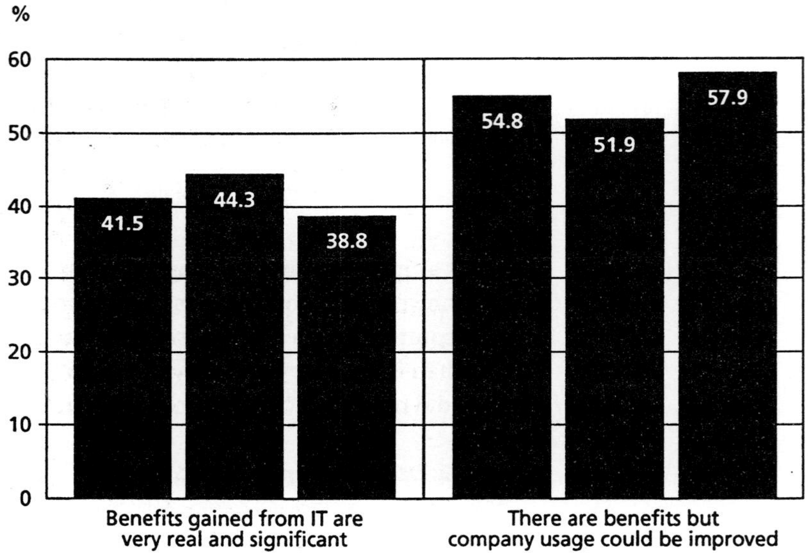

Although they said better use could be made of IT within their organisations, they were also aware of restrictions on its use (see Figure 4). Most people saw the time taken to set up and use IT to be the most significant drawback to IT (58.4 per cent), and more than half said that capital expenditure was a major consideration. The cost was often seen as an issue among departmental heads and managers. More than 33 per cent of respondents said they found 'difficulty of use' to be a drawback, and 23 per cent cited product training as a problem.

Figure 4: If you had to evaluate factors that might cause restrictions on the use of IT in your organisation, which of the following would be the most significant factor?

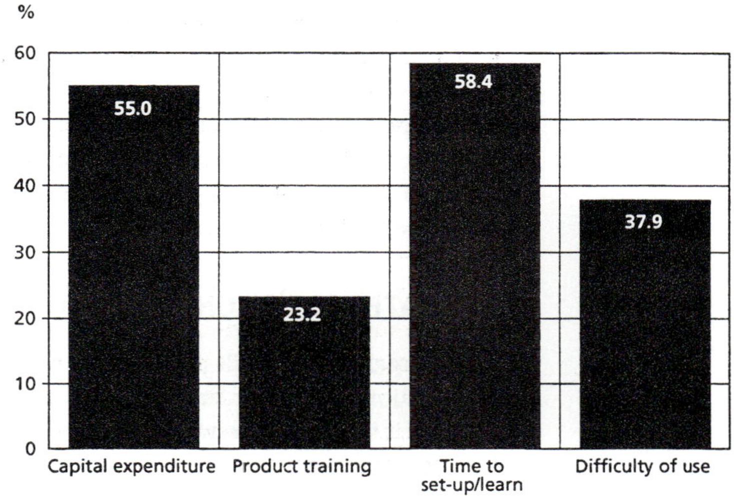

Despite these drawbacks, most respondents were happy with the software they have. Accounting packages were found to be reliable and easy to use, but lagged behind other applications in these qualities. Spreadsheet and word processing packages scored the highest for reliability, features and ease of use. For all applications, quality of support was found to be low.

More than half of the respondents said that they expected to re-evaluate their software within the next two years and cited reliability and performance as important considerations for purchasing new software. Windows capacity, including GUIs, and on-line access to datafiles also were found to be high priorities.

The survey showed that at least the management accountants within an organisation recognise and value the benefits of IT. More than 50 per cent cited 'accurate, up-to-date information' as the most important benefit that IT has brought to the profession. 'Improved and more flexible reporting' was also thought to be an important benefit, as was 'increased performance and profitability'.

Surprisingly, 'savings in time and cost', presumably a high priority of owners and managers, received a lower rating from management accountants.

And finally, few people continue to admit to being unconvinced about the benefits of IT: just a token 0.1 per cent claimed they could not see any benefits.

COMMENT

Here are the answers to the questions posed at the beginning of this section. Were there any surprises? Hopefully there was some 'comfort' factor to find that even four years ago, the actual use of IT was not as pervasive as might have first been assumed.

- 99 per cent + of management accountants do use a computer.
- Spreadsheets are the packages most used by management accountants, followed by accounting packages. Both databases and word processors had relatively little usage.
- Only 2 per cent of management accountants use an EIS more than any other package.
- Companies do not normally make management accounting information available to other departments because the information may not be relevant to other departments or it could be divisive.
- 40 per cent of respondents thought that the benefits from IT were significant.

- Restrictions on the use of IT include the time taken to set up IT applications and the capital cost of IT.
- Spreadsheets and word processors scored well regarding reliability and ease of use.
- The most important benefit from using IT is 'accurate and up-to-date information'.
- Only 0.1 per cent of management accountants see no benefit from the use of IT.

It appears that IT is here to stay. Remember that information management looks at the use of IT in terms of information, and not just the technology for its own sake. As you read any factual articles on IT, try to think of the information benefits that this technology will bring to a company.

1.3 LATERAL BENCHMARKING

Many organisations will assess their performance by comparing internal data with information on similar firms in the same industry. This process is extremely useful because it indicates how well (or badly) that organisation is performing compared with its direct competition. Also, the exercise is not limited to financial comparisons; almost any quantifiable item from refuelling time for aircraft to customer satisfaction can be included in the analysis. Because of this flexibility, benchmarking is a popular tool.

Although organisations do manage to obtain the necessary information to perform a benchmarking project, the analysis may be limited. The exercise will have the inherent assumption that the comparisons to be made will come from similar companies. So, where an organisation is already performing well, the benchmarking analysis simply confirms what is already known – that the organisation is performing well. Some additional information may therefore be useful so that a more detailed and meaningful analysis can be performed, in particular to find out where performance can still be improved.

The next article examines the use of information from organisations which are not in the same industry as a source of benchmarking analysis. Although this may initially seem to be an unusual move, the article clearly explains the benefits of the analysis and outlines some of the main pitfalls. Hopefully, this will provide you with some new ideas on how external information can be used to enhance the performance of different organisations.

LATERAL BENCHMARKING

Adrian Murdoch, *Management Today,* November 1997

Dallas-based Southwest Airlines used to have a problem. Most of its aircraft were on the ground between flights for an average of 40 – expensive – minutes. Although it had benchmarked its refuelling processes against other airlines, it found it was already one of the leaders. Some sort of quantum leap for improvement was needed, so it looked outside the airline industry for the most efficient refuellers in the world – Formula One racing. Adopting the turnaround processes used during pit stops, Southwest Airlines can now refuel an aeroplane in 12 minutes.

The tool which Southwest Airlines and many other companies are using to achieve this type of leap forward is benchmarking. It's an easy enough concept when that means measuring yourself against your direct competitors, but increasingly, companies are looking further afield and realising that to be the best means measuring yourself against the best in whatever sector and whichever country they may be found. It's an issue that is of vital interest to British businesses. A recent report from the Confederation of British Industry (CBI) put the increase in UK GDP were UK manufacturers to achieve US productivity levels at a staggering £60 billion. The report, *Fit for the Future,* also suggests that if the UK economy as a whole adopted US best practices, the increase in GDP could be around £300 billion.

And yet still all too few British companies have taken this lesson on board. In a report at the end of September, Partnership Sourcing – a joint venture between the CBI and the DTI – highlighted how few British companies have adopted benchmarking techniques. Of the 600 companies surveyed, 88 per cent were aware of the concept, yet only 62 per cent practised it. The take-up was particularly low among small and medium-sized enterprises.

As a management tool, benchmarking's canonisation began in the 70s with Xerox in the US attempting to beat off Japanese competition. The definition of David Kearns, former chief executive of Xerox, is still the best starting point: 'Benchmarking isn't just the hard measure of where someone else is, it's how they are doing it ... how the competition engineered the product to lower manufacturing cost.' But by benchmarking against best practice in other sectors and other countries, against the ABBs, the Motorolas, the Fedexes of the world, rather than just remaining within the industry, some companies are managing improvements in productivity and profits by leaps and bounds.

The mechanics of benchmarking are nothing new. The Greek philosopher Aristotle benchmarked various currencies to that of Athens in the fourth century BC, and at its most basic level that is what a stock exchange is – a benchmark of what a company is worth. Its value to a chief executive is that benchmarking along with business process re-engineering, total quality management and IT, is a tool, albeit a powerful one, that can be used for improvement. Michael Useem, professor of business management at Wharton, explains that there are two main reasons for benchmarking. First to establish best practice, and second to establish norms within the industry, for example pay levels. The most basic question for a company is how to get the benchmarkable data, which, as Mark Czarnecki, president of Houston-based consultants The Benchmarking Network, points out, 'falls into the grey area between the secret formula and public record'. Certainly Paul Ruggier, group quality director of Consolidated Finance Insurance at GE Capital, admits that it is 'the hardest task we have'. No one seriously considers industrial espionage, although one consultant dismisses what he calls 'competitive analysis' as 'low in quality'.

Essentially there are four methods that firms use to source this information. First, and most obviously, as Edward Collier, partner at Mercer Management Consultants, advises, use the information that you already have. 'Don't discount the information that is available for free – from the press, analysts' reports, annual reports and so on.' Second, listen to your people. 'With the service industries perhaps more than the primary or secondary industries, there is a high degree of staff turnover. If people move they bring new practices,' says Tony Burgess-Webb, head of international for public relations agency Hill and Knowlton. He gives the analogy of the early days in Silicon Valley when rapid turnover led to a swift dissemination of information.

Third, use consultancies. 'In the narrowest scenario take executive compensation. If you go to a consultancy it will sell you that information without naming names,' says Useem. More valuably, consultants can help you work round what seem like insurmountable problems. Werner Kreuz, European partner in charge of benchmarking for consultants AT Kearney, cites a two-part benchmarking study he was asked to do for a major British steel manufacturer. The first part was market benchmarking across seventeen European countries. 'It was easy to summarise the criteria on which decisions were based, even if the findings were different for each country.' The difficulty was part two – a cost-chain analysis for the company's nine major competitors. Naturally enough, if the consultants had asked for the cost chain of each of the firms, 'they would have kicked us out', but Kreuz identified that the yield was the critical factor in the cost chain, which the companies were, he says, 'proud to tell us'.

Fourth, ask others how they went about it. As Czarnecki points out: 'To talk of a payroll process as secret is foolish.' The question is often raised why companies would share data. Malcolm Graveling, partner at AT Kearney, sardonically suggests a Baldridge award syndrome – referring to the Malcolm Baldridge National Quality Awards in the US – where the winners want to show off why they are the best. It's good PR for them. Rob Garner, head of Rob Garner Ltd, who has more than a decade's experience with continuous improvement programmes at companies like ICL and Price Waterhouse, cites the construction company Mowlem, which is happy to share on the principle that by the time others have picked up on what it is doing it will have moved on. Others prefer to do it anonymously under the aegis of organisations like Price Waterhouse's Global Benchmarking Alliance, which for the last three years has been working with 60–70 global companies – like British Petroleum, BT and MCI. The most plausible answer, however, is that companies are selfish. They do it for what they can get out of it. Kreuz relates how ABB, in wanting to install a purchasing information system, set up what it calls a 'tiger team' to visit companies like Kawasaki Heavy Industry and Boeing, to see how others had done this within a decentralised organisation. The pay-off for the participants was that on completion they got to examine what ABB had developed.

That companies have to benchmark cross-sectorally to compete there is no doubt. We have moved a long way from Du Pont in the early 80s which only used to benchmark how far ahead of its competitors it was. Mark Rodriguez, vice-president of consultants ASM, follows the financial sector and admits that even banks – often the more conservative sector of the economy – realise they have to catch up and that to compare themselves solely with other banks is folly. When trying to convince clients of the value, he turns the question round: 'If I am General Motors, what can I learn from a bank ? Well, for many years now, both Ford and GM have earned huge revenues from fleet management of leasing and hire cars. If I am in that business, who am I leasing to? I have to learn how to segment the price on loans, evaluate and score customers. I have to look at the consumer banks.' While the more innovative companies have generated the impetus themselves, increasingly, pressure for change has been from the customer. With reference to call centres and customer helplines, John Gallagher, European director of market research at IBM, points out, 'The customer has a set of expectations and regardless of whether he's calling a bank, to order a computer, or calling about an auto offer, we don't have a different personal reaction.' This mirrors the findings of the Henley Centre's *Teleculture Futures* report published last year. 'Even if you are at the top of your class, if you don't believe that you can improve, then you are taking a risk,' he continues.

Cross-sectoral benchmarking, however, brings its own problems, not least of which is that of language. As Paul Pederson, partner and global leader of knowledge management at Price Waterhouse, points out: 'If you compare billing in the petroleum industry it is not that different from the accounts-payable process in other sectors.' Where he, naturally enough, sees the role of the consultants is that they can take the various outputs and 'map them back to a generic structure', and he talks of getting teams into a room to decide what to call the systems. Associated with this is how the data is presented, especially if a cross-border element is introduced. Much benchmark data – notably the Probe system commonly used across Europe – is given on a one-to-five scale. But Colin New, professor of manufacturing strategy at Cranfield Business School, points out that there is scope for error in some performance-related methodology. 'If, say, for delivery performance you get above 95 per cent you would automatically get a five [in some standard benchmarks]. However ideal that might be in the auto industry, if you did that for [a retailer dependent on fresh produce like] Tesco you would be out of business in five minutes.'

'You have to make sure that you are comparing apples with apples,' says Kreuz, explaining how he did this for a US chemical giant. The company wanted to compare its costs with its competitors. The greatest challenge in the assignment was not getting the information, but working out what every company deemed a cost, and how they had reached that figure. But even with benchmarking data on common ground there is still scope for error, and success comes down to judgement and implementation. While it may sound blindingly obvious, identifying the correct information among the data smog is one of the biggest issues for firms. As AMS's Rodriguez says, the greatest challenge for chief executives is judging which benchmark matters. Citing David Packard, the co-founder of Hewlett Packard, he quotes: 'More entrepreneurs die from indigestion than starvation.' A further difficulty is that firms often benchmark the wrong data, simply because it is easier. So firms end up doing something like a spend in procurement versus revenue benchmark instead. Then, says Czarnecki, although there is indeed very little that is non-benchmarkable, companies can take this to ridiculous extremes. They have to admit that certain processes within a firm are, if not industry specific, then industry-scale specific. It would be lunacy, says IBM's Gallagher, for a construction company to benchmark its cheque-payment process on a credit card company. 'It just doesn't make sense,' he says. 'If you are a credit card company you would look at firms with a similar scope and scale like insurance companies, banks or telephone companies.'

The greatest pitfall of all can be at the end – what to do with suggestions brought up by the data. As Wharton's Useem says, it is less than helpful to try and replicate another company's processes exactly. 'Observe and adapt and assimilate,' he says. 'Don't copy.' The chief executive has to use the information from the benchmark study in the appropriate manner and impart the aims clearly. Employed correctly, benchmarking can be used to get out of the Not Invented Here Syndrome as part of a change process. A common error, says Gamer, is for the company not to make clear the difference between the standard and the target. He cites the difficulty encountered by BT when it advertised that its aim was for nine out of ten telephone boxes to work. 'Engineers would fix 18 out of 20, and then call it a day. The target had become the standard.'

In terms of taking into account cultural differences when benchmarking, the camp is clearly split whether you need to or not. Ruggier is convinced that it would be impossible to implement exactly what works in Toyota in Wolfsburg [VW's headquarters]. You have to adapt to your culture and situation and business'. Useem, who would add corporate cultures to the list, points to the fact that no one has been able to get close to the customer focus that US retail store Nordstrom has, which he believes is 'embedded'. Poppycock, says AT Kearney's Graveling, disagreeing vehemently. Given that every process has an input or output, how can that be impossible to measure?

While that debate will continue, there are few who would now dispute that benchmarking is essential. The only question is where it will stop. Most believe that there is value to be had in benchmarking every part of the organisation. Certainly benchmarking studies are moving higher and higher into the more visible parts of the company such as communications and human resource departments. The trend seems to be, as Pederson has identified, for benchmarking to be done on a more long-range level and in directional trends. 'That is harder to map,' he admits, but as long as information can be presented which can help companies maintain a competitive edge, it will be used.

'We kicked off on the desktop with an international comparison,' says Duncan White, Scottish Power's executive director-multiutility, explaining how the power utility started its benchmarking process. 'We decided before privatisation [in 1991] that we wanted to grow, to do that we had to be the most efficient in the world.'

With the help of management consultants McKinsey, the company embarked on a three-month quantitative process with the Federal Energy Regulation Commission which has information on all the utilities in the US. It compared everything from customer service, generation costs, efficiency levels and maintenance issues to corporate overheads.

'The savings became instantly obvious. The group reckoned it could save around 25 per cent of controllable costs,' he says. After this, each business went out and looked at what others were doing in the field. The best-performing utilities that had been identified were visited, as were non-utilities, such as Fedex. The reason for going into the field was that 'cultural differences are not there, providing you go and see the processes on the ground. You have to recognise the environment you are working in.' 'White gives the example of Power Systems – the company's distribution and transmission arm – which went to Australia, Japan and the US. 'In Australia you don't have things rusting, the poles are wooden and their problems are ants. But you adapt the techniques,' says White. You have to look at issues such as whether it is time- or need-based maintenance, for example. Similarly, Scottish Power went to benchmark Japanese utility Kyusho Electric Power Company, which has the lowest customer minutes lost in the world – apart from typhoons, customers are off supply for four minutes a year. Although the infrastructure is different, in that Japan uses wires rather than cabling, 'we took the principles of live-line working back', says White. Scottish Power says that it is on track to reduce times by 20 per cent. 'We're now at 68 minutes from 77. We're aiming for 55.' The core point for White about benchmarking is that the company sits down and works through the information it has gleaned so that it can benefit operationally and financially. Power Systems alone has saved £20 million. 'If it's benchmarking for benchmarking's sake you can spend your life trawling the world. We've had two years of implementation and now we're about to up the ante again.'

1.4 INFORMATION FOR STRATEGIC MANAGEMENT

Strategic management require information at a strategic level, that is, in summary format, with important items highlighted etc. This format of information helps managers to quickly and efficiently assimilate what they are being given, and should therefore lead to timely decision-making. The information required would normally be obtained from two main sources: internal to and external from the organisation.

One major barrier to the production of this type of information used to be cost. In many situations the detailed internal operational information would be available, but reformatting this into summary strategic information could be a costly process. Even with computers to produce totals of sales, additional work could be needed to achieve the level of variance analysis required. More time input would then be required to place this into the appropriate report format for managers to read.

Obtaining appropriate external data could require an even larger time input. There would be no precise system in-house for obtaining the information, so collection would tend to be a very *ad hoc* process of obtaining competitors' accounts, products or press releases, and then checking other sources like government or trade associations occasionally. Allocating time to obtaining his information was like trying to measure the proverbial piece of string – there was always more information than could be collected in the time allowed.

The ability to obtain information has been made a great deal easier by the increased use of information technology over the last few years. The changes may not have been particularly significant regarding the actual collection of internal information, although there are now more powerful presentation packages available to display the information in appropriate formats. The use of organisation-wide intranets also means that more information can be accessed by any individual, though they are not yet in general use.

But for external information, the ease with which details have become available from the WWW is amazing. Most organisations now have their own Web sites and, while some information like product development will still be secret, obtaining copies of past accounts or in some cases detailed product specifications are only a few mouse clicks away.

For both internal and external information, the main message is 'more is better' – that is, enhanced computer technology allows more information to be produced and makes accessing and summarising that information easier. More strategic information is becoming available and so managers are facing information overload. The problem now for managers is no longer deciding how much time to invest getting the information, the problem is how to sift through the information to find the bits that they actually need.

In this article, Taylor and Graham investigate:

- whether information that is being provided to users is actually meeting their needs;
- where information could be obtained, particularly for strategic management;
- whether information is in the appropriate format for managers.

Although this article was written before the expansion of the Internet and intranets, it is interesting to see that managers were starting to face information overload then. For many managers, the situation must be much worse now!

INFORMATION FOR STRATEGIC MANAGEMENT

Brian Taylor and Craig Graham, *Management Accounting*, January 1992

In today's business environment every executive needs to react quickly. Businesses are facing increasingly complex markets, customers and suppliers, and fierce global competitive pressures. In order to make the right decisions more quickly, senior executives must have focused, high-value information to improve the speed and quality of decision-making and enhance the performance of their business. The information must help the executive formulate and review strategy in addition to monitoring ongoing performance.

As management accountants, the provision of information to the top levels of our businesses is most often our responsibility – what is our record in meeting the needs of the senior executives of our companies?

Does the information we provide meet its users' needs?

The evidence from several studies shows that the information needs of the executive boards of UK companies are not being met. 'Drowning in information, but starved for knowledge'[1] summarises one of the biggest frustrations for executives today. The traditional huge monthly pack, even if accurate, gives the executive very little chance of verifying the accuracy. Poor presentation militates against ease of interpretation and its late arrival means the chances of the executive acting upon it and making good decisions is therefore remote.

The KPMG survey of information for strategic management[2] highlights other areas of concern – it shows that information currently provided to executive boards is biased towards financial indicators and concentrates on internal self-determined comparisons. The majority of respondents rated the information available to formulate and review strategy as poor or average and a considerable number stated that it failed to highlight critical issues.

In general the survey shows that information provided for strategic planning and control gives senior executives only a narrow view of the business as it provides them with insufficient information on non-financial and external factors.

Consequences

What are the consequences of not meeting the information needs of your senior executives? By providing primarily internal financial information executives tend to concentrate on operations, rather than policy and direction. Most successful changes in company direction are triggered by quickly reacting to external events, such as changing consumer tastes.

The failure of information provided to senior executives to have an adequate external orientation and not focus on issues that will impact on the business will lead to a slow-moving organisation with competitors stealing a march. An over-simplified but most relevant adage is that 'good companies follow indicators, bad companies follow the crowd'.

If information is not provided in a consistent and focused format it will lead to disagreement and confusion at senior levels. Without focus there will be conflicting signals. This again slows the decision-making process as it is left to the board to sift to find the information they need to concentrate on.

A further consequence of information not highlighting the crucial issues is that important board-level decisions are based on hunches and feelings, rather than hard facts. Decisions based on hunches are not in themselves a failing but they must be underpinned by at least a good general knowledge of all the internal and external issues.

In summary, the consequences from executive boards not using the right information are a laborious, ill-informed decision-making process, missed opportunities and consequently lower profits.

How should the information set be developed?

In order to meet the information needs of your executives the information must:

- enable them to monitor and control the organisation's activities in a manner measurable against its strategy and objectives;
- contribute to the strategic decision-making process.

One of the most commonly used methodologies for developing the information set against these two factors is to match it to the critical success factors of the business. Critical success factors are 'the limited number of areas in which results, if they are satisfactory, will ensure successful competitive performance'.[3] The most common factors cited by executives as being crucial to the success of their business are:[4]

- cost structure;
- product quality and innovation;
- customer satisfaction;
- management development;
- change management and flexibility.

You can see that information concentrating on financial control will only be concerned with cost structure – and your own cost structure at that – yet senior executives need information across the entire range of critical factors. In what has become known as world-class manufacturing, the orientation of performance measurement has shifted radically towards the explicit measurement and reporting of non-financial factors. Further, the recognition of human resources and management skills as major assets requiring investment means that progressive companies monitor these areas as well.

What information should be provided?

Figure 1 compares traditional management information with information for strategic management. Information for strategic management includes financial information but must also include non-financial information such as project management and human resources information. Also it should not just come from the financial reporting unit at the end of each month. For example, project management information should be reported against milestone dates rather than monthly and should be presented in a complete format which may need, for example, finance and marketing departments working closely together to produce what is required.

Figure 1: Sources of information for strategic management

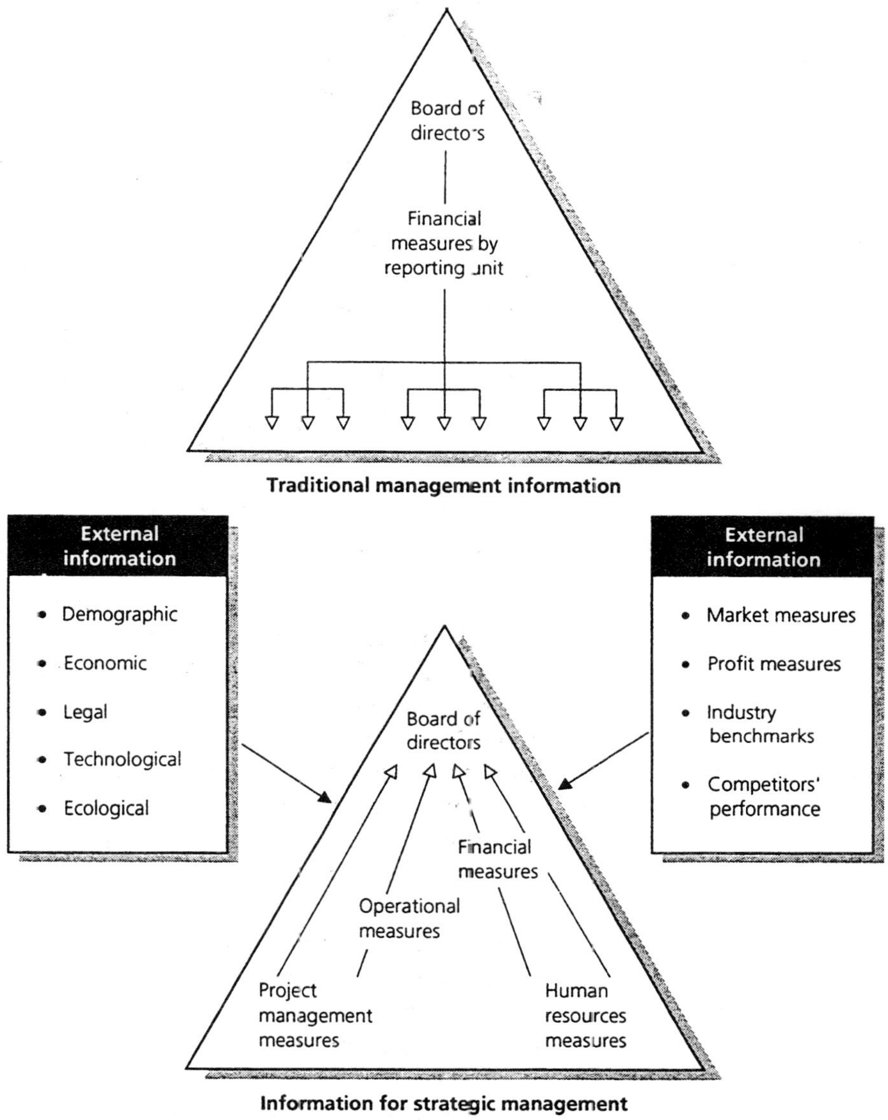

Figure 1 shows that traditional management information tends to be primarily internal whereas the information set required should include a broad range of relevant external information varying from general economic indicators to specific competitor and industry benchmarks. At the top of the organisation senior executives are only interested in a summarised view of the organisation's internal performance but place heavy importance on external information. This is true in practice but it is alarming how few senior executives focus neither on competitive measures of performance nor on factors which will affect their operating environment. In order to formulate and review strategy, executives must concentrate on external factors. Success is measured on performance against these factors rather than only against own past performance.

Figure 2 provides the framework for, and some examples of, the information which should be provided to senior management executives.[1] Traditional management information concentrates on the upper left quadrant of the framework, internal financial information. At an operational level this may be all that is required but at board level the information provided must span the entire range of financial, non-financial, internal and external information. The relevant external and non-financial information will vary both by industry and even by company within each industry. It is, of course, most dependent on your selected strategy.

Figure 2: A framework for information

		Internal		External	
		Past	Future	Past	Future
Financial	Numeric	Management accounting	Budgets and forecasts	Competitor's results	Brokers' forecasts
	Text	Results narrative	5-year plan framework	Brokers' review	Press opinion
Non-Financial	Numeric	Operating performance	Capacity planning	Market share	Market research
	Text	Performance commentary	Strategic goals	Trade media coverage	Technology forecasts

In what format should the information be provided?

By recommending that the information set covers the entire information framework we are in danger of only aggravating the problems of information overload; however, by focusing on high-value, relevant information this danger should be minimised. This is most often done by concentrating on key performance indicators. These are the limited number of indicators which measure business performance against your key objectives and industry benchmarks. The information set is most often developed from the key performance indicators, thus retaining focus on objectives and the critical success factors of the business.

The use of an executive information system provides an excellent presentation medium. It can provide fast access to the information and present it in a format which is both meaningful and easy to digest. Effective use of an executive information system means that the executive can spend more time on interpretation, decision-making and problem-solving and less time on analysis and requesting additional information.

What benefits will be achieved from effective information?

Senior executives who have critically reviewed and improved the information they receive have benefited in a number of areas of business performance. These include increased market share, better control of projects against their milestones and improved communication at board level. All the benefits are underpinned by having the right information available quickly, enabling executives to react swiftly to take opportunities or to defend themselves from threats.

The benefits achievable from providing improved information to senior executives are often difficult to predict and quantify financially, yet the chief executives of many companies have cited improved information as a major contributor to improved profitability. In addition they also acknowledge a crisper insight into strategic goals, developing a common understanding of what is important for the success of the business and how this should be achieved. A chief executive of one of the newly privatised water companies has also stated that the use of an executive information system to provide focused, relevant information has facilitated a move towards flat management structures by cutting out the need for information filters.

The case studies describe two cases where the information used by board-level executives was inappropriate, was affecting the financial performance of the company and had to be reviewed and improved.

Case Study 1 – Construction Industry

The housebuilding subsidiary of a large international construction company started making heavy losses after many years of increased profits. The recession had started to bite and the disappointing results, although expected, were worse than anticipated.

This forced the executive board of the subsidiary to review the information it was using for strategic planning and control. For the first time they started to concentrate on external information, in particular the financial performance of their competitors and economic indicators.

The competitor analysis showed that, despite profits increasing annually and surpassing targets, their own company had still been under-performing their construction industry competitors. As a result, when recession hit the market, they were one of the first companies to suffer.

The analysis of economic indicators had showed that in the period before the depression house prices had been outstripping disposable income at a rate which was matched only by the period before the 1970s house price slump. Such growth, if projected forward, was unsustainable yet the company and the subsidiary had ignored this information when formulating strategy and buying land.

The information forced the subsidiary and the parent company to reformulate their corporate strategy and objectives and redefine the information set provided to senior executives.

The early signs are promising:

- the executives are confident with the well-defined, focused information set they are using as the basis for strategic decision-making, and
- the long-term financial performance of the subsidiary is improving and is now catching up with its competitors.

Case Study 2 – Retail Industry

A high-street retailer was operating in a niche market with its strategy based on selling high-margin quality products.

The company's market share was never very high but it started to decline. At this time the finance director was carrying out a review of board-level information prior to installing an EIS. The current board information pack concentrated on internal information; external information provided at board level was done on an unstructured, *ad hoc* basis and was often out of date by the time the special exercise was completed.

The finance director produced an information set which focused on the company objective of selling high-margin quality products. His external information included, for example:

Financial information:

- Competitors' sales analysis and total market size
- Economic indicators such as disposable incomes, inflation and demography
- Supplier profitability and market share

Non-financial information:

- Number of repeat sales
- Number of customer complaints and faulty products returned
- Press reviews of products
- Advances in technology

The non-financial information did not look at the company's products in isolation but looked at all competitors and products in the market-place.

The provision of competitor strategy and product information helped to identify the cause of the falling market share. The competition had been slowly increasing the perceived quality of their products using improved packaging and branding and the company's competitive advantage was being eroded.

This information became the basis for formulating future strategy. After considering future trends in customer spending habits and advances in technology, the company decided to retain its objective of selling quality products but decided to redesign and relaunch the range. By constantly updating and reviewing the information set it considers that it will now always be able to identify and react quickly to its external environment.

Conclusion

Information is the lifeblood of organisations, yet the information provided to our most senior executives has failed to match their requirements for swift decision-making. By matching board-level reporting to the company's strategy and objectives, information becomes much more meaningful for both strategy formulation and performance monitoring. By producing focused internal and external, financial and non-financial information companies can improve their decision-making and thus their competitive position.

1. David Harvey and Ian Meiklejohn: *The Executive Information Systems Report.* Business Intelligence, 1990.
2. KPMG Management Consultants: *A Survey of Leading Companies 1990 – Information for Strategic Management,* 1990 (0171-236 8000).
3. York Freud: *Planning Review,* July/August, 1988.
4. *Winter: Index Indications.* Index Group/KPMG, 1983.

1.5 DOES THE SPEND JUSTIFY THE MEANS?

Although the next article was written in the context of accountancy firms, the principles can be applied to any non-manufacturing organisation. The problem being addressed is a relatively simple one: how do you know that investment in IT is a success?

The question is easy to state, but very difficult to answer. In a manufacturing environment, capital investment can be measured in terms of changes in productivity per employee or falling price per unit manufactured. Other measures such as ROI, ROCE or even payback will also be applied to determine the 'success' or otherwise of the investment. However, finding the appropriate measures or information sources to show whether these measures have been achieved in non-manufacturing situations can be much more difficult. With IT investment, the direct effect on productivity may be difficult to determine (what is a 'unit' of production anyway?), and in a non-manufacturing situation, price is determined on the service provided, not on the amount of materials used or necessarily the time taken to produce an item. Additional measurement problems will be introduced where the organisation does not maintain adequate records of the computer expenditure.

The solution would appear to be twofold: firstly, to maintain appropriate accounting information of the IT investment, and secondly, to change the criteria being used to justify it in the first place. In many situations, the full costs of IT investment are not recorded, hence appraisal is difficult. Collecting all costs including hardware, software, consumables, training, new office equipment etc. will be necessary to any appraisal decision. Similarly, if the investment has no direct effect on productivity, then other measures can be used to justify the expenditure. The next article provides some ideas of the criteria that can be used, including the expenditure making some benefit to the overall strategy of the organisation. At the end of the day, there may be no easy solution to the problem of justifying IT expenditure. However, showing that the investment does actually help the organisation will provide some measure of comfort where IT expenditure on non-manufacturing situations is involved.

DOES THE SPEND JUSTIFY THE MEANS?
Kevin Kan, *Accountancy SA*, July 1996

Many IT personnel in accountancy firms face the daunting task of justifying their request for IT expenditure or IT budget increases. In addition, IT partners face scrutiny by their fellow partners over such expenditure. Naturally, any decision to invest in IT must benefit the firm. So how does a firm make IT investment decisions, knowing that it impacts on the firm's efficiency, productivity and income?

Survey findings

An interesting finding from the survey is that the more IT-literate partners in accountancy firms were, the more likely they were to invest in IT projects/proposals.

What's more, younger accountants and graduates ranked highly in terms of IT knowledge compared with other staff. This most likely reflects the increased information systems education taught at undergraduate level. It may also reflect the reason for the conservatism in IT investment thus far.

All firms surveyed believed that they recouped their IT investment. However, only one firm was actively measuring its return/productivity on investment. Most firms found it difficult to measure both tangible and intangible returns on their investments.

What should we do?

To help make it easier to justify IT expenditures to partners, proposals should include the following:

- cost of the project
- how the project fits into the practice's objectives
- expected return on the project
- impact on revenue/bottom line
- effect on the practice
- effect on the staff
- measurement of benefit from the project.

When putting together a proposal, it is important to ensure that the expenditure is aligned with the long-term goals of the firm as well as to ensure that the expenditure is aligned with the existing IT strategy (i.e. it is no use buying an Apple Mac when the rest of the office is using IBM compatibles, even though the Apple has better desktop publishing facilities). It is essential to get feedback from the users when putting together the proposals since the users are the ones that will be the most affected. In particular:

- what effect does this expenditure have on them?
- do they get job enrichment?
- do they learn new skills?
- are they going to lose their jobs?
- is retraining needed?

These are the intangible measures that are not easily measured yet they have an impact on the IT investment proposals. One way to justify IT expenditure/projects is to determine your IT portfolio. What does IT comprise of in your practice?

The IT portfolio must balance the risk of the investment with the benefits that it generates and whether it meets the practice's objectives. This can be quickly summarised in pyramid form:

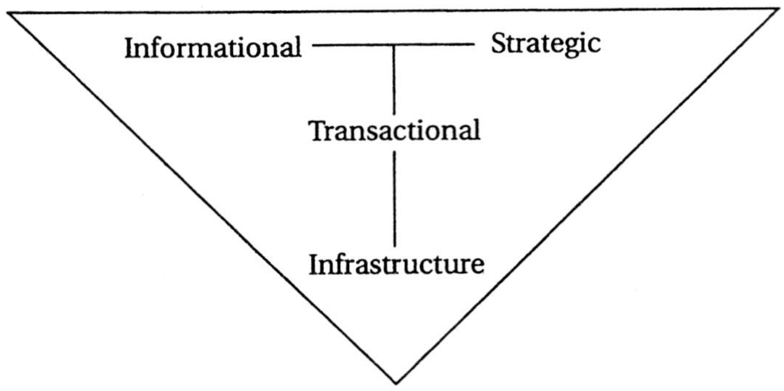

Using the pyramid is quite simple. Which part of the pyramid does the IT expenditure fall in? Is it Infrastructure? Can we continue to build on this in the future, (e.g. hardware purchases)? Is it Transactional? Can we reduce the cost of data capture? Is it Informational? Can reporting be enhanced from the system either to manage the practice or to give better information to clients? Is it Strategy? Can a competitive advantage be obtained with this investment?

Strategic investments are the most risky, and many firms will not spend a great deal in this area due to their conservative nature. Should a firm make an IT investment in this area, it will ensure it acquires a leading edge and it will possibly spend a great deal more to stay in front of the pack. Most investment will be in the areas of infrastructure (the platform a firm will use), transactional (software that reduces the cost of data capture) and informational (the ability to improve reports to help management and clients make better decisions).

Another method of justifying IT proposals is the balanced scorecard (see *Harvard Business Review*, Sept/Oct 1993, p.134). This has a dual purpose in helping firms determine whether they have met their objectives and is also a method of measure. If an IT proposal can fit an objective listed in the scorecard, it may help to get it justified. The scorecard is designed to help firms achieve breakthrough improvements in critical areas like customer and employee satisfaction, financial impact and market development.

The scorecard has its biggest impact on organisations when it is used as a driving force for change. Should firms need to embark on major organisational change such as implementing new computer systems, the scorecard would be a good tool to use.

The scorecard ideally suits an accountancy firm as it requires input from the different business units to see if they meet the overall corporate objectives.

Implementation issues

The survey also showed the importance of a staged IT implementation. Most firms were practical enough to realise that they require staff to be efficient and productive through a period of change. This is why a staged IT implementation is important. It allows staff to be trained properly and to become familiar with the new system before embarking on more changes.

Also, having a staged IT implementation allows you to measure whether the IT project has delivered its intended benefits.

Measurement

A simple measure could be the increase in fees generated by the IT investment. However, this is difficult to determine due to external factors such as the economy and competition or marketing strategies which may not show a clear picture.

Some firms pointed out that if a tax return was completed in five minutes less time per return, this was a satisfactory measurement; staff were therefore spending less time doing compliance work and they were able to do more in less time. Other firms believed that intangibles such as staff morale, job enrichment and streamlined job procedures were the measures they needed in terms of IT investment.

What the survey pointed out is that intangibles are difficult to measure but they play an important role in the measurement of IT investments.

Other considerations

The surveyed firms did not have a set IT training budget. Rather, they saw IT training as part of an overall training budget. There is nothing necessarily wrong with this except to say that the budget may be used for other things like the latest tax training or the latest accounting standards training – which does not leave much for IT training.

Although many firms believe that they have the in-house expertise to look after their IT investment, outsourcing the maintenance or development of their systems is a viable option. When new issues or products arrive, a lot of time is spent by internal IT staff in coming to grips with the new issues.

It is just as cost-effective either to send the IT personnel to training or to get the external IT supplier to come in to train or tailor the system to meet your needs. This way, you can reduce the amount of downtime to your practice and any anxieties that may eventuate.

This expenditure on outsourcing may be only a fraction of the opportunity cost of prolonged downtime to a firm. Consequently, any reduction in opportunity cost to the practice must mean benefits and savings to the firm.

Conclusions

The survey shows that firms see business value in their IT investments. They believed their IT investment had been recouped and that they had a competitive advantage in terms of their IT investment. However, they also believe that if this investment is not maintained, they would lag behind other firms. Most firms view IT as a prerequisite for success.

Measures of the return on IT investments are important. However, the effect IT investments have on the organisation must be considered: analysis is required of the impact these investments have on the organisation in terms of the effect on staff and the impact on efficiency, productivity and the quality of work produced for clients.

It is also clear that firms need to beef up their IT strategy with regard to their IT justification plans. Only one firm surveyed was able to detail in depth its IT strategy and the check points that must be passed before an IT proposal was accepted.

Firms may need to have a look at techniques such as the IT investment pyramid and the balanced scorecard as a mechanism to help justify IT expenditure and to ensure that any investment meets the overall firm objectives.

IT has delivered significant changes and benefits to the business world – and to the accountancy profession in particular. The days of typing tax returns in triplicate are long gone. Undoubtedly, many firms have seen the business value from their IT investment, but like any investment it requires regular reviews to ensure that you get the best return.

1.6 A SOURCE OF COMPETITIVE ADVANTAGE?

Accurate, relevant and up-to-date information is essential to the survival of any organisation. However, many organisations may fail to provide this information to their decision-makers, not deliberately, but more as a result of a 'historical accident'. In other words, information systems tend to grow with the organisation and, while they will change and adapt with that growth, there may be no strategic review of the systems to ensure that the necessary information is still being produced. The information may appear to be accurate, relevant etc. and may well serve management purposes; however, a detailed review of the systems would suggest that some improvements are required.

Another possible problem with the information being produced by internal systems is the lack of breadth of the information being produced. Many accounting systems can produce excellent financial and management-related data and the numeric output from those systems can be manipulated and displayed in many permutations. The point is that the output is numeric and internally focused. Although some accountants may like the output for precisely this reason, providing additional information like reasons for variances of actions or competitors could significantly enhance the standard of the output.

Furthermore, information may be focused on to one functional area of the organisation. A problem in one department such as production may result in an adverse variance in another department, such as sales. For example, substituting a poorer-quality material may result in a higher returns variance due to the sub-standard material. If the purchasing and sales functional areas are not linked, then the underlying reason for this variance may not be accurately identified.

In the situations outlined above, decision-makers may not query the output from the information system, simply because they are not aware of any better alternative. The question is how to justify any change when the information system appears to be producing what is required and decision-makers have not requested any improvements.

This article examines in more detail the problems that can arise when information systems grow with an organisation without any real review, and then moves on to suggest how to effect some useful change in those systems. The main areas where amendments to information systems are justified revolve around either increasing the competitive advantage of the organisation or assisting the organisation in meeting its corporate objectives. This is not to say that the authorisation for the change will be easy to obtain. But, as Clive Lewis shows in the article, there are methods that can be used to assist the process.

A SOURCE OF COMPETITIVE ADVANTAGE?

Clive Lewis, *Management Accounting,* January 1993

In a survey recently conducted by Coopers & Lybrand, the single most important reason given for changing management information systems was 'strategic'. This was closely followed by 'to remain competitive'. Less formal surveys and straw polls strongly suggest that management information remains, for many, the single most important issue on their management agenda.

This article suggests that a large part of the problem lies in over-reliance on financial information, an unclear view of alternatives and lack of a process systematically to improve management information.

Traditional management information

For many organisations, management information, mainly financial, has evolved over time. Very often the vast majority of the data comes from the financial ledgers. The supporting rationale has been that in order to make meaningful comparisons between cost centres, profit centres, business units and indeed companies, it is necessary to express everything in financial terms.

Add to this the fact that the production of management information is nearly always entrusted to the finance director, then the bias towards financial information is hardly surprising. However, our surveys and our experience suggests that many companies view as inadequate the information with which they currently manage their businesses. *The problems with organisations' management information* are many and varied. Some of these may be familiar:

- information does not support business priorities;
- important information hidden in a maze of detail;
- information too late to be useful;
- everything expressed in financial terms;
- information structured to reflect the organisational structure, not the activities and processes.

Management information should form the vital link between an organisation's strategic objectives and its business performance. It can only do this if real management responsibility is closely linked to the information provided.

An expanded perspective

Over many years Coopers & Lybrand has worked with a variety of organisations to help them to develop more useful management information. While recognising that every organisation's requirements are different, there are some common elements that represent best practice in the area of management information; it should be balanced, relevant and consistent.

Balanced information means including information from a number of different perspectives. A balanced view will typically include these perspectives:

Financial – this will continue to be a crucial measure of overall success, although greater focus should enable a much reduced volume of data to be used.

Customer – seeing your own performance through the customer's eyes is increasingly recognised as an important way to ensure that performance in key areas is up to the required standard.

External environment – the need to monitor and understand the dynamics of the business and competitive environment is more important now than ever.

Processes and activities – by understanding processes and their constituent activities, organisations can highlight areas of concern and focus attention and action accordingly.

Continuous improvement – how well an organisation and its people are learning and developing is crucial to its long-term competitiveness. However, few companies systematically monitor how well they are actually doing this.

Management needs a BALANCED view of all factors affecting performance

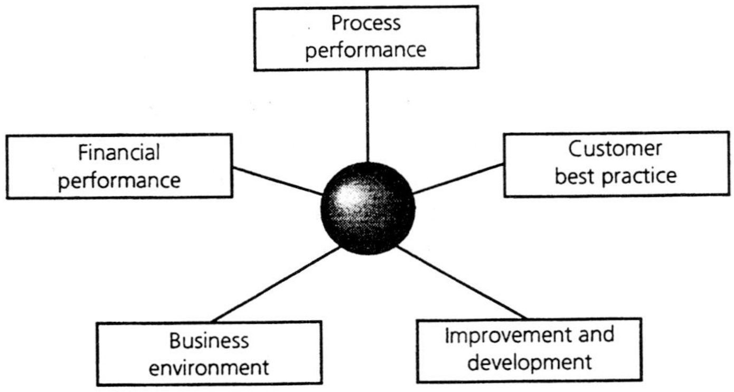

The second element to our view of best practice is that information should be relevant.

All too often information is arranged solely according to the organisation structure that is in place. However, the reality for most organisations is that many processes cut across several functions. Since it is processes and their activities that in fact translate an organisation's strategy into business performance, management information needs to reflect processes and activities at least as much as it reflects the organisation structure.

The final element of best practice is that information must be consistent.

The dictum 'What gets measured gets done' is a widely recognised truth. To express it somewhat differently: consistent performance measures lead to consistent performance.

The starting-point for consistent performance measures must be what it is that the organisation is trying to achieve. These objectives can be translated into critical success factors and then down the hierarchy into functions and processes and ultimately into activities.

Performance measures need to reflect and support this hierarchy. By explicitly recognising the relationship between each of the levels it is possible to construct a management information structure that helps to ensure that it is the critical activities which are the ones that get done.

Why organisations are reluctant to change

Because management information has often evolved with the organisation, the need to change does not always appear to be compelling. The comfort of having too much information and, very often, a small army of management accountants and others to provide analysis and additional information, outweighs the vague notion that the information they really should be focusing on is not readily available.

It will often take a shock of some sort for a company to be forced into action. Typically a financial crisis or perhaps intensifying competition will force a company to recognise that it does not know which levers to pull to correct its problems. It is then that organisations begin to recognise that instead of being the source of competitive advantage that it should be, their management information has for too long failed to help them to focus on what is really important for their success.

Obstacles

One often overlooked reason for reluctance to change is the fact that management information, even if it is inadequate, will often underpin existing organisation structures. Challenging and changing performance measures and making very visible individual managers' responsibilities and accountabilities can be very unsettling to the managers concerned. Even if old measures are demonstrably outdated or irrelevant, they may remain very attractive to an individual if they show that the individual is doing his job 'well'! A process to confront issues of this sort is extremely important.

Another difficult obstacle to overcome is that many organisations are cynical about the improvements that can be made to their management information. They will have tried to make improvements in the past which have resulted in little more than the addition of graphics and commentary to existing information. Without adopting a fundamentally different approach, it is not surprising that only marginal improvements are made.

As a key management process that should be at the heart of what an organisation is trying to achieve, making lasting changes demands commitment and takes time.

RELEVANT measures support management by both function and process

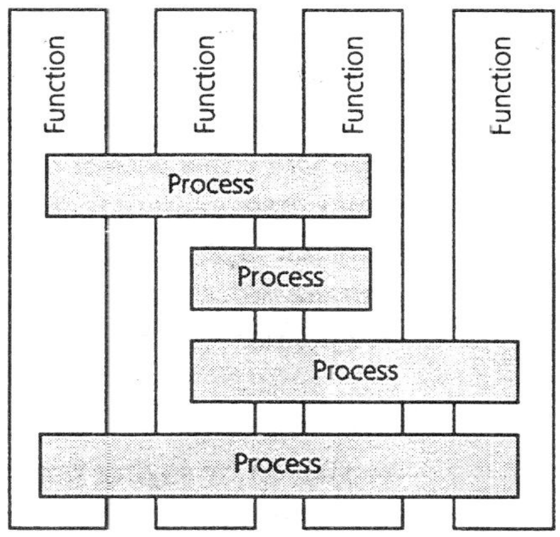

Measures for lower levels should be CONSISTENT with those which drive senior management

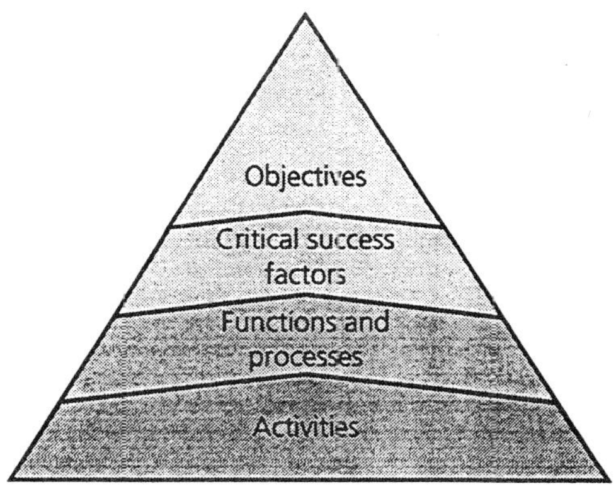

A process

Effecting fundamental change also requires that there is a robust process in place that not only helps companies to define their requirements, but also addresses all of the objections and barriers that are likely to come between an organisation and the real benefits that it can gain from improved management information.

We have developed an approach called 'Strategic Business Information' which we have successfully used with many companies to define and implement step change improvements to their management information.

It has been our experience that a process needs to be comprehensive and structured, but extremely flexible. This is because it is nearly always the case that projects to improve management information do not arise simply from a perceived weakness in existing information. Rather, they arise from a recognition of the role that better management information can play in improving business performance. Very often we find that organisations will link a number of initiatives aimed at performance improvement, to work being done to improve their management information. It is very important that any process used is flexible enough to ensure that the potential synergies of running more than one improvement project are in fact realised.

The strategic business information approach takes as its starting-point the organisation's or the business unit's strategy and objectives. It then goes on to define explicitly the organisation's critical success factors before linking them to all of the underlying functions, processes and activities. Key to the success of the process is the clear assignment of responsibilities to ensure unambiguous management responsibility for all processes and activities, even where these cut across functional boundaries. Performance indicators and measures are defined at each level in the organisation using the three best practice elements referred to above – balanced, relevant and consistent.

The approach is controlled and 'owned' throughout by the organisation concerned. Experience has shown us that without genuine and sustained commitment from the senior management team, either the project will run out of steam or the benefits will fail to match expectations. The role of the external consultant is usually to provide support with the process and specialist input in tackling specific issues or in challenging existing viewpoints.

Summary

We started by saying that traditional management information often fails to support what an organisation is trying to do. We have presented here an expanded perspective on what management information can look like and discussed how, when properly defined and implemented, it can be a crucially important part of an organisation's armoury.

Chapter 2

Information Systems

2.1 INTRODUCTION

Information for decision-makers has to be provided by a variety of information systems within a organisation. This chapter looks at how those systems are established, and in particular, how to ensure that the overall organisation strategy is supported by the information systems, rather than the system and the information that it provides driving the organisation.

The articles in this section are:

- 'Risk and management of information systems' – trying to assess the risk attached to implementation of a new IT system.
- 'IT drives the chair' – looks at the area of IT and the information produced by the system providing some form of competitive advantage to the organisation.
- 'The French connection' – a case study on Air France's use of information technology.
- 'Why lawyers can't wait' – a different view on the year 2000 problem focusing on the legal aspects rather than the IT problems of that date.

2.2 RISK AND THE MANAGEMENT OF INFORMATION SYSTEMS

One of the main problems with implementing new information systems is the risk that the system will not provide the benefits required or meet the expectations of the users of that system. This problem can be particularly acute with IT systems because there is often a very limited amount of testing that can be performed on the system before it goes live. Similarly, it is likely that the amount of user involvement will be limited simply because it is difficult to prototype a whole system, or because the user interface may be so different from existing procedures that trials would result in mainly negative feedback.

The author of the first article in this section contends that applying risk management principles to the implementation of IT systems can produce significant benefits both in terms of decreased risk of implementing an incorrect system and in ensuring user acceptance of the system. These objectives are achieved by identifying the main reasons why an IT project can fail, and then ensuring that these 'fail criteria' are not present in the project currently under review. Implementation of some form of risk management can therefore be very beneficial to an organisation.

This article was actually written as a prelude to a CIMA Mastercourse workshop on risk management. More information on risk management can therefore be obtained by attending this workshop.

RISK AND THE MANAGEMENT OF INFORMATION SYSTEMS

Dan Remenyi, *Management Accounting*, February 1997

Despite an infamously high failure rate, the risks associated with information systems are regularly underestimated, if not totally ignored. The reason for this is that information systems risk is a challenging concept to define, to understand and ultimately to manage. Furthermore, not many managers or organisations go to the trouble to master this important aspect of information systems management.

One of the reasons that contribute to this is the fact that risk can mean different things to different people. Historically, risk is defined as the possibility that the actual input variables and the outcomes may vary from those originally estimated. This implies that the extent of the possible difference between the actualities and expected value reflects the magnitude of the risk. Although the word 'risk' is usually seen in the context of a potential hazard, or the possibility of an unfortunate outcome resulting from a given action, intrinsically risk may be either positive or negative. Thus, for example, projects may finish either early or late, or be under or over budget. None the less, when information systems professionals talk about risk it is almost always in terms of what can go wrong.

Of course, the concept of risk has been used by general management who, traditionally, have identified two main components associated with risk – business risk and financial risk. These two components are combined in order to assess the total risk of the firm or the enterprise. Information systems risks need to be considered differently. One approach to categorising them has been supplied by Professor Warren McFarlan of Harvard Business School, who suggests that there are two main categories of information systems risk, which are described as risks associated with failures of execution and risks caused by failures of conceptualisation.

The risk associated with failures of execution can be categorised under three headings: the risks related to the structuredness of a project, the degree to which a project incorporates company-specific technology, and the size of the project. The structuredness of a project refers to the completeness of the definition of the end outputs of the project. Projects with a high degree of structuredness would incorporate such examples as the automation of existing forms, where the original layout was to be maintained. Such projects would be, from the point of view of structuredness, low-risk exercises.

Projects which utilise a high degree of generally new, or company-specific new, technology entail higher amounts of risk. This is typical of business process re-engineering (BPR) projects. These increased risks should be weighted against the dramatic benefits that it is hoped the project will realise. According to the McFarlan view the project's size is the final category of risk. Simply stated, projects which cost one million pounds have inherently greater risk than projects which cost one thousand pounds.

In general IT-based BPR projects will entail rather large investments. They will often use technology with which the organisation will not necessarily be familiar, such as moving from centralised mainframe computing to client-server architecture, and will sometimes address applications which have a relatively low degree of structuredness. Thus risk identification and management is certainly an important issue in BPR projects.

Failures of conceptualisation are simply ideas which were not likely to succeed from the beginning. It is possible to identify a number of main categories of projects which will generally fail due to poor conceptualisation:

1. A project which fails to meet a customer's needs, no matter how technically sophisticated it is, is setting itself up to fail. Technology can perform wonders, but if there is no market for the products or services the project will fail.

2. The intended system may require behaviour which is not ingrained in existing users, such as the use of terminals. As people generally shy away from change, such a system which requires change will fail.
3. Projects which are easy to replicate will also fail, as competition thrives on timely duplication of simple innovative ideas.
4. Systems incapable of evolving will fail. Evolution is an essential aspect of survival in the dynamic business environment of the modern commercial world.
5. If the system is highly interoperable with other systems, users may see it as a commodity and swap to the cheapest vendor of that commodity. Hence there is definitely a place for proprietary systems in the modern business environment.
6. Technology can be a two-edged sword. As well as providing competitive advantage it can lower entry barriers by reducing the costs of competing. If the project's ideas are rejected by the customer's culture then it will fail.
7. Projects that are undertaken before all the strategic pieces are in place are going to fail. It is important to set up the alliances that are necessary before undertaking the project.

The issues described here as articulated by McFarlan are useful as a framework for thinking about risk and information systems, but they do not lead directly to an approach for the management of information systems risks. For this, risk management is required.

Risk management may be defined as the art of recognising the existence of direct or indirect threats, the determination of their consequences on resources, and the application of modifying factors or courses of action in a cost-effective way to keep these adverse consequences within controlled bounds.

Risk management involves a separate set of activities which are not at present generally undertaken in many organisations. Risk management is essentially a financial issue. The financial implications of the risk occurring need to be quantified and this provides a budget for a risk prevention programme.

Recent research suggests that risk management should be an ongoing process and not just a one-off exercise. Thus it is necessary to formulate a risk management strategy which should be implemented by project managers who are close to the detail of the work being conducted. Furthermore, it is necessary for risk management to continue throughout the life of a project.

Research also indicates that those information systems managers and their colleagues who have adopted the principles of risk management have been able to demonstrate clear benefits. These include reductions in the waste of resources in the development of information systems and the delivery of more complete information systems on time and within budget. It is clear that the principles of risk management when applied correctly can produce significant paybacks for organisations implementing information systems.

2.3 IT DRIVES THE CHAIR

Some developments in the IT infrastructure can help organisations improve the speed with which information is moved around the organisation. For example, a simple e-mail link will allow departments in different locations, or even different countries, to send messages and documents to each other in the space of minutes rather than days using a postal service. Similarly, computer systems can be used to monitor stock levels in shops and electronic data interchange used to reorder goods that are selling quickly directly from suppliers rather than sending paper-based orders in the post. Cutting down the reorder time also means that inventory levels can be reduced with a consequent saving in storage space and decrease in working capital requirements.

However, speeding up the transfer of information is not an objective in its own right; organisations must be able to use this increased speed in some way to provide some benefit or competitive advantage. The last paragraph provides two fairly obvious examples of how organisations can put this enhanced information flow to good use. As new technological products become available which provide even more sophisticated information exchange options, the challenge for most organisations will be finding appropriate uses for them.

In seeking to find these new uses, organisations will have to avoid the IT tail wagging the organisation dog, while at the same time ensuring that some competitive advantage can be obtained from the technology. One area that many organisations may well investigate is Efficient Customer Response (ECR) which is a shorthand way of saying that an organisation can try to use the enhanced information to provide better customer service. As the next article explains, this is certainly the case in the retail sector where large databases about the spending habits of customers are being accumulated. Most supermarkets now issue some form or affinity card, which is used by the consumer to accumulate 'points' towards various awards. However, the supermarket can collect information on individual customers to identify spending patterns. Personalised 'money-off' vouchers can be sent to each customer based on that consumer's spending habits to try to increase the business at that particular store. This can be seen as a way of providing ECR – in that consumers appear to be receiving a benefit from the technology, although the organisation is also receiving a larger benefit.

In the next article the area of ECR is examined in more detail and more examples are given to show how technology can be used by different organisations to try to achieve competitive advantage in some form. Although the title may be 'IT drives the chair', the article looks at the ongoing race in many organisations to keep ahead of their competitors by effective use of their newer technology.

IT DRIVES THE CHAIR

Malcolm Wheatley, *Management Today*, November 1996

Exciting new technologies in logistics were once to do with physical distribution: racking systems, trucks and automated warehouses. These days, the buzz surrounds the use of IT in logistics. While the development partly reflects diminishing marginal returns in the physical handling technologies, it also illustrates IT's emergence as a tool for both data handling and communication. With today's emphasis on logistics within the entire supply chain, communication of pieces of information as diverse as demand patterns, vehicle locations and inventory quantities is vital.

Expenditure on logistics-related IT applications has therefore been rising sharply, and software and hardware companies have been battling to claim their slice of the market. According to conference organiser Andrea Murphy, over 40 per cent of the exhibitors at Logistics 96 this October offered IT solutions of one description or another, be it hardware, software, data communications equipment or systems integration services. What's more, 'the distinction is blurring', she notes. 'IT capability is being built into everything from automated materials handling systems to forklift trucks.'

Consequently, points out Rob Morgan, director of supply chain re-engineering at management consultants KPMG, the IT-related costs borne by industry have been rising. He estimates that a new entrant, needing to develop a logistics capability from scratch, would find that 20–30 per cent of the costs of the overall logistics infrastructure was represented by IT-based items. 'IT is now a significant logistics enabler,' he adds. 'It's a real competitive differentiator.'

But how? Where exactly does that extra competitive edge come from? The answer depends upon your perspective. IT certainly has a growing role within business at a micro level, aided by mobile data communications. Automated warehouses, once a fashion that looked set to give way to more flexible approaches, are now seeing a new lease of life as businesses realise that they can link them to forklift trucks and stock control systems. Vehicle fleets can be made more responsive with in-cab data terminals that direct drivers to their next delivery or collection point, and print out error-free documentation on the spot.

However, it is at the macro level, across the supply chain as a whole, that IT is seen as offering businesses the greatest opportunities. According to Dr Ian Canadine, director-general of the Institute of Logistics, businesses are seeking what he describes as 'the control room concept'. 'Blue-chip companies are becoming very serious about large integrated logistics systems,' he notes. 'They want to know what is going on throughout their entire supply chains – to be able to predict the consequences of a ship slowing down somewhere in the Mediterranean, or of a disruption in the supply of components from Japan.'

Systems suppliers are therefore seeing strong demand from companies wanting such control, particularly those operating on a multinational and multilocation basis. The task before them is complex since it frequently calls for transactions to take place in several languages and currencies, and for inventories and production pipelines to be visible to users thousands of miles away.

German software giant SAP's R/2 and R/3 software products have for a long time been virtually the only software serving this market, despite a reputation for complex and expensive implementation procedures. For a long time, the only real alternative was writing one's own software. Companies such as Hewlett Packard did this over 10 years ago, but now it, in common with many others, is phasing the system out in favour of an SAP solution that 'plugs some of the gaps from which the old system suffered', according to logistics manager Gilbert Celli.

The objective, he explains, is for the company to be able to take an order in one country, deliver it to another, and (if necessary) invoice in a third currency.

The principal medium for achieving this is electronic communication through electronic data interchange (EDI) rather than the faxes upon which the company relied before. Orders are transmitted from dealers across Europe to a central demand collation point in Germany, and thence – instantly – to the various factories and distribution and configuration-postponement centres around Europe that will meet the demand. Back down the line will flash a message indicating the anticipated delivery date. The message is sent days before it would have been despatched under the old system, and by the time it is sent, schedules and material call-offs have already been put in place to meet the commitment.

'The whole point of technologies such as EDI, e-mail, electronic point of sale (EPOS) and barcoding is that they don't have to mimic paper-based processes,' says Colin Billinge of GE Information Services. Retail chain Tesco, he notes, has achieved a steep change in productivity through a range of initiatives based on EDI. 'Stock turns have increased from 13 to 36 times per year, while customer service levels have risen from 92 per cent to 98 per cent.' Overhauling its logistics function, focusing largely on the role of IT, has enabled another GE customer, Motorola, to slash procurement lead times from 40 days to one day, and cut warehousing space requirements by 50 per cent.

But attention is already shifting from simple EDI to a wider approach that aims to link together a number of new technologies under an umbrella of cross-company co-operation. Efficient consumer response, or ECR – the search for technology-led advantage in the supply chain – is currently attracting a huge amount of attention in the grocery industry. If successful, it should prove a model for other, less efficient industries.

At its heart lies a switch in corporate strategies away from the adversarial approaches that currently cripple the efficiency of most supply chains. For if every link in the supply chain fully implemented technologies only patchily implemented so far (such as cross-docking, automated store ordering from EPOS data, barcoding, and electronic funds transfer), considerable gains could accrue. According to the ECR Europe Executive Board, a group of suppliers and manufacturers who are interested in the technique, $27 billion (£17.3 billion) a year could be cut from the cost of Europe's food retailing supply chains through the combined effect of an estimated likely 4.8 per cent reduction in operating costs, and a 0.9 per cent reduction in inventory costs.

Despite the enthusiastic reception that ECR is receiving – instead of the 300 delegates expected to attend a recent conference on the subject, 1,200 turned up, and 300 were reportedly turned away – the actual adoption of ECR is proceeding more slowly than some of its proponents would have wished. 'There are some barriers,' acknowledges Philip de la Chambre, head of Coopers & Lybrand's ECR consulting practice. A basic lack of understanding of ECR's objectives is one such difficulty.

Another, more serious, problem is a lack of empathy with ECR's objectives. Co-operation is vital for ECR to work, and undue exertion of power or abuses of participants' relative positions simply 'destroy the potential gains'. Likewise, cross-functional politicking within companies can also damage the fragile bridge-building process.

But the most intractable problem is ECR's heavy reliance on systems that extend along the length of the supply chain; it means that what de la Chambre describes as 'differences in maturity' constrain the chain to the capability of the least sophisticated link. Likewise, much of the potential of EDI and barcoding is wasted unless it extends right across the supply chain: isolated islands of excellence are likely to do little on their own.

Unfortunately, an ECR feasibility study carried out on behalf of the ECR Europe Executive Board serves chiefly to highlight gaps in the supply chain. Although every company covered in the study was implementing at least some ECR principles, the average overall maturity score achieved by manufacturers was just 35 per cent – in other words, they were little more than a third of the way towards achieving full ECR. Retailers scored little better, with an average score of 42 per cent. What's more, for both manufacturers and retailers, 'a broad spread existed between the most advanced and least advanced companies'.

Much of the change in attitude required has to come from retailers, whose rapacious approach to cost-cutting has encouraged the present-day adversarial culture of the food industry supply chain. The next year or so will show whether they have the breadth of vision to overcome these difficulties; if they do not, then ECR is unlikely to spread from its current tentative beachhead. One sobering thought should encourage retailers, however. In the US, where ECR first emerged, retailers are not only grappling with the same issues but also fighting off a threat from nascent home-shopping vendors, who, by capitalising on the very technologies that lie behind ECR, offer doorstep delivery without incurring the trouble and expense of operating stores.

2.4 THE FRENCH CONNECTION

Almost all organisations establish their IT infrastructure to help them meet their information requirements. For example, if your organisation is a supermarket, then the IT infrastructure will provide information on the goods in stock for inventory control, and hopefully on customers so that their buying habits can be determined. Similarly, if your organisation needs to move information around the world quickly and cheaply, then different methods of moving this information will be investigated and an appropriate IT solution implemented.

The point is that the information requirements normally drive the implementation of the IT infrastructure itself – very few organisations will spend millions of pounds on an IT project and then see how it fits into the overall business strategy. The only exception to this rule might be where a significant IT investment is needed to meet a given information requirement and the only method of doing this is to leave spare capacity in that IT system. For example, an organisation may need a WAN to deliver information to a large number of locations, while at the same time allowing for a significant increase in the potential throughput of data. A small investment would not meet this need, so a large investment is required leaving excess capacity in the organisation. However, some excess capacity now may well pay dividends in the future when this capacity will be used.

Given the rapid pace of change in computer systems in recent years, leaving some spare capacity may be a wise move. It was only in 1990 that the Acorn Archimedes computer with two megabytes of RAM and no hard disk was considered a reasonably powerful home computer. Today, the standard amount of RAM is ten times larger; all computers have a hard disk as well as other accessories like CD-ROM drives and modems. The apparent 'spare capacity' in two megabytes of RAM lasted only one or two years.

Having excess capacity means that it could be used to generate additional income, if an appropriate buyer of the capacity can be found. However, the strategy of effectively selling part of the organisation's main IT system to a third party is potentially risky. What if, after having got the third party on board, the customer then wants to make changes to the system to meet its own requirements? And what about the basic question of customer service? If your organisation does not have the skills in this area then do you employ yet another third party to provide service to the other? The bottom line is that control of the IT system could be turned away from providing the information that your organisation requires to servicing the requirements of the third parties. This is not a situation that many organisations would want.

The next article is a case study based on Air France. Here, Peirs Ford examines how Air France successfully managed to do what has been discussed above, namely sell some spare capacity on a WAN while still keeping control of the IT resource to meet its own information requirements. This is an excellent case study to show how diversification can be achieved in organisations, even though this was not the original objective of an investment.

THE FRENCH CONNECTION
Piers Ford, *Corporate IT Strategy,* February 1996

In these competitive times, most organisations are heavily preoccupied with how they can add value to their core business and services. That value can take many shapes and forms. Even so, the notion of one of the world's largest airline companies taking on a national telephone operator and offering value added data services to a host of prospective new customers doesn't spring readily to mind. After all, if British Airways has ever considered taking on BT, it's kept very quiet about its intentions. However, that is exactly what Air France has set out to do with its new wide area network. By the end of the century, the airline conservatively expects to have snared 6 per cent of the French data communications business, worth FFr600 million, and putting it second only to France's national carrier, France Telecom.

Of course, France's profile has been high in recent months. Controversy surrounding its nuclear tests has been matched by international interest in its survival of a prolonged public sector strike. But Air France's telecommunications operations division, having been through the rigours of privatisation, has sailed serenely through the initial phases of establishing one of the largest WANS in France, the backbone of which should be fully operational by the middle of this year.

Philippe Balin, Air France's telecommunications director, said that potential customers always ask about the likely impact of a strike on services. 'The answer is that in the past, yes, a strike would have mattered,' he said. 'But for now and in the future, a strike only affects France Telecom. We've already had the revolution and striking is behind us.'

What, then, lies behind Air France's decision to become a telecomms operator and offer dedicated data communications services to its customers? The impetus seems to have come from the top. Balin said: 'Our president's idea is that we have to diversify. Clearly, the majority of Air France is concerned with the airline business, which may be independently profitable. But we also have value added telecommunication operations, and it would be a pity not to invest in that and sell our services if we can compete in that market.'

Air France's private international telecommunications network dates back to 1968, when it started out as a heavily proprietary, if powerful, configuration. In 1985, it took the decision to migrate to a network based on the old TDM standard technology, using Ascom Timeplex and Northern Telecom products, but investment ceased in 1992 while the organisation took stock for the future. In 1995, it opted to integrate that network with a backbone based on the emerging high-speed network technology ATM, supplied by Stratacom.

The combination of many years' experience in telecommunications with some of the most advanced technology available today makes Air France, on paper at least, a formidable competitor in the services market. As Balin said: 'We have a role to play in the French market because we have such a well-established, important network. That is why France Telecom considers us to be its main competitor. As an airline, we have to be on top of the technology. Certainly, that should be attractive to our external customers. But our main customer is Air France itself. Our first need was to reduce costs while providing a more powerful network to meet the needs of the airline. We had to be able to offer a high-quality service and real-time operations.'

In fact, Air France's request for tenders to create the new network was a daunting document, requiring the successful applicant to guarantee payback on the equipment within two years and a ten-year lifetime for the technology.

'Air France doesn't have a great deal of money to invest in this activity, but investment in data communications needn't be high,' said Balin. 'You can do a lot with FF100 million. We had to use our existing network and use our customers to finance the investment. Obviously, our main investment is in planes, not telecommunications, because we are an airline. But because we already had such a significant network, the money needed to invest in it and win new customers isn't necessarily so great.'

Certainly the implementation of the new WAN seems to have gone remarkably smoothly, not least in terms of the time taken for Air France's network team to get up to speed on the new technology. According to Balin, they took just one week to take control of the network.

Balin stressed the close links between the airline's activities and the reliability of the network itself. For example, it had to accommodate a new generation of client/server applications as the airline migrated from its existing mainframe systems. Once these requirements had been satisfied, the way was clear to use the network to capitalise on the blossoming data services market.

However, the ability to offer a sophisticated range of turnkey solutions to its customers does not alone guarantee Air France's success as a telecomms operator. One of the main challenges it faces is to convince the market that an airline can also be a reliable provider of data services. Balin conceded that there is an image problem which can't necessarily be solved overnight.

'There is an ambiguity,' he said. 'But it is our true intention to become an important supplier of telecomms services. There is no doubt about the quality of our network. If customers buy a connection to our network it will work. But the question mark lies over Air France's future as a telecomms services provider. We have to work with our customers to show them it isn't just a short-term operation. We began this activity in mid-1995 and we have already signed up more than fifteen customers. We think that's a good start, but we have to continue and there is a lot of work to do. Thanks to media coverage, more people now see us as a telecommunications provider. We receive between one and three requests for tender every day.'

Air France's new network aims to capitalise on the expected explosion in French demand based on the high-speed frame relay network technology, especially for interconnecting multiple local area networks. Balin is convinced that there is a market in France for dedicated networks among customers who want the benefits of networking without having to invest heavily in it or operate and manage it themselves. Air France's traditional customer base for telecomms services has been in markets closely associated with the airline industry. At the start of 1995, this was worth some FFr120 million per year to the organisation. Balin said: 'Now, we have to focus on all kinds of customer, not just those linked with the airline business.' He is convinced that Air France's long years of experience in private networking will be advantageous. 'That means, when we are in discussion with the customer, we have a good understanding of what they want and why they want it. Their problems have been our problems in the past. We don't want to sell on a tariff basis. We want to customise our solution to meet the customer's requirements.'

Air France retains realistic ambitions rather than aiming for world domination. That's probably wise. Deregulation in France is not very advanced and France Telecom's monopoly is underpinned with some very powerful resources. For example, Balin said that there is no intention for the airline to extend its datacomms interests into the voice market. It also expects to work closely with other suppliers rather than monopolising its customers and actively encourages them to source products and services from more than one supplier. 'We have set ourselves a realistic target, although we obviously hope to do better than that,' said Balin. 'How much better depends on the culture of the telcomms management in our customer sites. We try to train our customers to have several suppliers. Why not share the load between France Telecom and Air France if you can reduce your costs that way? But we have some work to do on that point.'

He added: 'Today, our private network covers all of Europe, North Africa, the US, Canada, Mexico and some countries in the Indian Ocean region. We have five nodes in the UK. But our first priority is in France, and with customers who also want international connections. For example, we wouldn't accept a request for tender which only required connections in the UK.'

Air France's telecommunications business is a classic example of a potentially lucrative business emerging from an organisation's existing resources. The investment in the new wide area network was driven by the company's own internal requirements, but the network clearly has the capacity to become a significant finance-generating business in its own right. It's the ideal outcome for any IT department which has survived the transition from internal resource to independent cost centre, meeting market forces head-on. *Vive la différence!*

2.5 RE-ENGINEERING YOUR ACCOUNTING

The year 2000 problem is receiving more and more attention. Many articles seek to explain the problem in terms of hardware and software, noting the fact that computer systems will fail and data loss will result on the first day of the year 2000. Given the fact that all companies rely on computer systems to some extent, the risk of loss affecting any individual organisation appears to be significant.

You may expect that an article on year 2000 in an information management publication would focus on the actual loss of information within a system. This is not the case in this book. Although the likelihood of loss is high, as noted above, the actual loss is very difficult to determine because it is related to the actual software being used. Articles which examine specific 'fixes' for different software types do not, therefore, seem to be appropriate. This publication therefore includes an article on the legal aspects of ensuring year 2000 compliance. What employees and directors should be doing now to try to stop data loss and the legal consequences of not doing this are quite serious. However, these points are easy to miss because the focus in on the software, not on the bigger picture of liability.

This article on year 2000 compliance therefore focuses on the necessity to take action from a legal point of view, rather than approaching the problem from maintaining the integrity of the organisation's information systems. Potential legal liability appears to extend not only to the companies manufacturing software, but also to certain individuals within organisations who purchased that software. So, if you are a company director or manager of an NHS trust, you may be advised to pay particular attention to the threat of personal liability!

WHY LAWYERS CAN'T WAIT

Judith Oliver, *Management Today,* October 1997

British industry is treating the millennium time bomb issue with cavalier complacency. So say the experts who warn of dire business consequences for those whose computer systems fail to master the change from the year 1999 to the year 2000. 'Some businessmen still seem to view this whole issue as a joke,' says Robin Guenier, executive director of Taskforce 2000, a government-backed organisation set up to raise awareness of the issue. 'But it may not seem so funny when their business fails and they are held personally liable for its losses.'

To date, much of the debate about the year 2000 problem has dwelt either upon the Armageddon scenario of worldwide business collapse or on eye-catching estimates of the colossal costs involved. (Experts estimate that fixing the problem will cost £31 billion in the UK and $1.5 trillion worldwide.) Now attention is turning to more prosaic concerns. In America, a small supermarket owner in Michigan is bringing the world's first lawsuit over the millennium time bomb.

Tec-America, the Atlanta-based supplier of cash registers, is being sued for allegedly providing computerised tills that cannot recognise the year 2000. Countless other computer systems worldwide are predicted to crash on 1 January 2000, if not before. And businesses will certainly fail as a result. So who is going to be liable, and for what? And, when the writs start flying, as Guenier insists they will, could any of them land in the laps of company directors themselves'

Lawyers are bracing themselves for a busy few years ahead. Rob McCallough of international legal firm Masons anticipates a rapid rise in the dispute work surrounding year 2000 issues. 'Views are mixed about how much there will be,' he says. 'But certainly in the States, a great deal are expected.' And it's not just the suppliers of mainframe computers who could be facing law suits. Karl Fielder, head of Chichester-based year 2000 consultancy Greenwich Mean Time, has investigated the year 2000 status of 4,000 best-selling PC software programs. Almost two-thirds of them, he claims, will run into problems in 2000. Yet, of these, 28 per cent are claimed by their manufacturers to be year 2000-compliant (i.e. neither performance nor functionality is affected by dates prior to, during and after the year 2000). Fielder concludes that many companies, particularly the small and medium-sized ones, are currently using software which won't input dates after 31 December 1999.

All year 2000 problems can be fixed through software updates, technical tinkering or the purchase of new systems (average costs range from £400 for a small firm to upgrade or replace software to £300 per employee for larger organisations). But time is running out – for many experts a realistic deadline for fixing the problem is the end of 1998, and for some industries which work far ahead it is even earlier. Relying on insurance to cover any costs incurred by systems which fail to master the millennium date change is not an option. Year 2000 insurance cover is very costly: at present £100 million of cover costs £80 million – and, says Charles Henderson of global insurance brokers Willis Corroon, many insurers are now considering changing the terms of their policies to exclude any year 2000 liability.

Many companies will be relying on their IT supplier – although IBM in particular has come under fire for concentrating its efforts on mainframe users and not being proactive in alerting its smaller users to the problem. At Sage, the world's largest PC accounting software supplier, public relations manager Georgina Cameron admits: 'Some of our older products are not currently compliant.' However, she insists the company is committed to contacting all 180,000 UK customers over the next six months to assess their year 2000 requirements and to ensure their Sage accounting software is compliant. Free upgrades will be offered to all 100,000 customers who subscribe to Sagecover – Sage's maintenance programme. The rest, says Cameron, will be offered solutions at a nominal charge.

But what if IT suppliers refuse to play ball? What about taking them to court? If the product concerned is a new one, your chances of success are good. Due to the efforts of organisations such as Taskforce 2000, awareness of century date-change problems is now widespread. All new software should he genuinely 2000-compliant. If not, consumers can seek protection under general consumer legislation such as the Sale of Goods Act 1979 and the Supply of Goods and Services Act 1982. The former allows goods to he returned on the grounds that they are not fit for the purpose they were bought for, or they are not of satisfactory quality. Unless a supplier states otherwise at the time the sale is made, software bought in 1997 which fails to master the date change cannot he considered fit for purpose.

For companies using existing custom-built software and hardware or standard packages and computer systems, however, the legal waters are muddier. In these cases, says Peter Stevens, partner in charge of the information technology group at leading City law firm Manches & Co., much will depend on the wording of the contract or warranty. 'If there is an express warranty or agreement concerning 2000-compliancy then the user has an unequivocal right to sue the supplier for breach of contract,' he says. Even if there isn't, a court may judge that an implied warranty exists although it is likely that the supplier would argue otherwise.

One point on which there is likely to he much debate is the exact date after which software manufacturers may have been reasonably expected to supply only year 2000-compliant programs. While 1995 is frequently quoted by industry pundits as the reasonable cut-off point, the British courts have yet to make a judgment. Until that date is established, users will find it hard to know the strength of their own case. Moreover, as McCallough explains: 'Although the courts may seek to impose an objective test as to when it was best industry practice to supply year 2000-compliant software, each case will be determined on its own facts.'

Another important consideration will be the use to which the product has been put. For example, a supplier of software may argue that, used on its own, the package was fit for purpose. It was only when it was linked with other packages that problems occurred. As Gavin Pickering of law firm Radcliffes Crossman Black explains: 'Unless a user specified at the time of purchase which other products he intended to use the package with, it may prove very difficult to establish a claim.' Microsoft, for example, insists that all its software products are 'ready for the year 2000' but refuses to provide warranties to this effect – a decision it justifies in a recent release with the following explanation: 'Contractual warranties specific to year 2000 readiness are not appropriate given the true nature of year 2000 issues and the simple fact that a single technology provider cannot solve all issues related to the transition to the year 2000.'

Microsoft isn't the only company to write exclusion clauses into its warranties – whether they will stand up in court, however, is another matter. Potential litigants may find some comfort in the Unfair Contract Terms Act 1977, which aims to exclude limitations which are not 'reasonable'. But, warns Fielder, 'the major suppliers have enormous funds available to fight these types of claims. It scarcely seems likely that small companies will have the clout required to wage protracted legal battles against the industry big boys and win.'

The time for taking legal action may also be rather more limited than many people might think. 'Those wishing to sue for breach of contract must bring the action within six years of the date of the breach,' explains McCallough. 'In terms of suing for noncompliant software, the limit is therefore six years from the date of supply, not from the time the problems occur.' If, on the other hand, the user chooses to sue for negligence, actions must begin six years from the date that damage occurs. Negligence, however, can be trickier to prove than breach of contract.

Even if a company has what appears to be an otherwise cast-iron case against a supplier, it will have to show that it did all it could to mitigate any loss by taking the proper steps to deal with the problem before the year 2000 deadline. 'Any plaintiff has a duty to try to mitigate his loss,' says Pickering. 'He can't just blunder on and wait for damage to occur in the belief that he has a claim against the supplier. Attempts must be made to limit the damage.' Failure to do so could substantially reduce the level of damages awarded.

A client company which fails to do all it can to deal with the problem may also find itself on the receiving end of legal action. For example, if it fails to supply goods or services due to computer failure, its customers could sue for breach of contract. While the unfortunate supplier may try to claim *force majeure*, i.e. that it was impossible to fulfil the contract, the courts may dismiss this claim on the grounds that the cause was not outside their 'reasonable control' but could have been avoided by taking adequate steps to ensure that their computer systems were year 2000-ready.

An even more worrying aspect for company directors is that they could be held personally liable if their company fails because of a year 2000-related computer problem. 'There is no doubt that directors are going to he sued over failure to contain the year 2000 problem,' insists Pickering. 'If it is not already here, the point will come soon where directors will be presumed to know they should have done something to fix the problem. From that point onwards directors are going to be liable and it will take only one example to set the scene for many claims against them.' And since practically anything with an embedded chip is now under suspicion, including security systems and medical equipment, that could even mean criminal charges. According to a report in *Computing* magazine, NHS trust bosses could face manslaughter charges if chips, such as those in life-support systems, fail and cause fatalities.

Directors are therefore advised to keep a record of the action they are currently taking to address year 2000 problems, in case any claims are made against them. A first step is to audit all the company's current date-dependent systems and examine all the relevant warranties and contracts. Any future contracts should include clauses on millennium compliance. 'The purpose of looking at liability at this stage is to see how strong the cards in your hand are when negotiating with suppliers or consultants,' says Robin Baron of Radcliffes Crossman Black. Ultimately, he says, organisations will have to look for someone to blame, but that time may not yet have arrived. 'The vital thing right now is to get these problems solved. If the problem isn't solved by the millennium, then it probably is not going to be solved at all. Fix now, sue later – is the message.'

Useful Web Sites / Sources of further information

- **www.sage.com** Sage's site which includes Sage's year 2000 policy statement and will maintain a year 2000 knowledge base to be updated with relevant information
- **www.bcs.org.uk/millen.htm** British Computer Society site. Includes an overview of the year 2000 problem, plus links to other useful sites
- **www.year2000.com** Year 2000 Information Centre site, co-sponsored by Peter de Jager, one of the world's leading year 2000 experts
- **www.bsi.org.uk** British Standards Institute site. Includes the BSI's Definition of the Year 2000 Conformity Requirements
- **www.open.gov.uk/ccta/mill/mbhome.htm** Site of the Central Computer and Telecommunications Agency (CCTA), the government's IT agency. Includes guidelines aimed at helping organisations tackle the year 2000 problem
- **www.taskforce2000.co.uk** Taskforce 2000 is a government-backed body directed by the heads of the Confederation of British Industry (CBI) and the Computer Software and Services Association (CSSA) to raise awareness of the year 2000 problem
- **www.ncc.co.uk/y2k.html** National Computing Centre site offers a number of products and services to assist organisations in addressing the year 2000 issue
- **www.microsoft.com** Microsoft's home page
- **www.novell.com** Novell's home page
- **www.software.ibm.com/year 2000/index.html** IBM's year 2000 support centre
- **www.cssa.co.uk/cssa** Site of the Computing Services and Software Association, trade association for the UK's software and IT industries
- **www.computerexperts.co.uk** Site of Computer Experts, producers of the Millennium Bug Toolkit
- **www.rightime.com** Site of RightTime, producers of various toolkits for Year 2000 auditing. Also includes links to many other related sites
- **www.gmt-2000.com** Site of Greenwich Mean Time, producers of the Check 2000 auditing tools

Chapter 3

Management Information Systems

3.1 INTRODUCTION

Management information systems are one of the main delivery systems for the information that managers require. This chapter looks at some of the types of MIS available and the information that they provide. The last few articles also look at Internets and intranets and the potential business application of these information systems.

The articles in this section are:

- 'Management information systems to support a world-class company' – looks at the information that is needed to ensure that the MIS can provide a complete output.
- 'Data warehousing' – the first of two articles on this subject. The first article concentrates on the structure and software used in the warehouse.
- 'We've got the information somewhere but ...' – continues the investigation of data warehouses from the point of view of the uses of the information contained in the warehouse.
- 'Executive information systems: not just for executives any more!' – shows the benefits of letting all staff access and use information on an EIS.
- 'The Internet – the Swiss army knife of business tools' – shows some of the benefits of using the Internet for individual organisations.
- 'Intra, not Inter!' – looks at intranets as compared with the Internet and considers the benefits of this information product.
- 'Internet customer service' – provides some case studies on how the Internet has been used to enhance customer service in some organisations.

3.2 MISs TO SUPPORT A WORLD-CLASS COMPANY

Information, particularly information being used by more senior managers, will normally be provided by some form of management information system (MIS). In general terms, an MIS must provide accurate, timely and relevant information to those managers that require it. How the MIS collects and then provides the information is not normally an issue that managers will concern themselves with. As long as the information meets their requirements, then they will, on the whole, be happy.

It is useful to investigate exactly what information the MIS should provide and in general terms how the MIS should be structured to provide this information. The next article looks at these two areas. In general terms, an MIS must provide information to help managers ensure that the organisation's mission and objectives are met. Managers can therefore review performance of the organisation using the MIS information and compare this with the goals that the organisation wants to achieve. Action can be taken to correct any deviations found.

In establishing the MIS to meet this objective, care must also be taken to ensure that all sources of information are included in it. It will be of little use to provide internal production data unless some indication of external demand for products is also given. High production is irrelevant if no sales can be achieved! The output from the MIS can also be varied depending on the type of organisation or system being supported. The article provides an explanation of some possible objectives of an organisation and shows how the MIS can be adapted to provide relevant output to meet these structures.

The second area investigated is the actual structure of an MIS, which depends partly on the type of output required, although there will always be common areas of input to provide the tailored output. The main areas of input will include:

- Information from the organisation's other information systems such as accounting, production etc.;
- External information on competitors and consumers of the organisations' products;
- External information on the general state of the economy and in particular on the market in which the organisation is operating;
- Details of the objectives of the organisation with links to the other sources of information to show how these objectives are being met.

How the inputs are combined to provide the appropriate output depends on the individual organisation. However, as noted above, the information provided must assist the managers in checking that the organisation is meeting its objectives.

MANAGEMENT INFORMATION TO SUPPORT A WORLD-CLASS COMPANY

Kevin G. Dilton-Hill, *Accountancy SA*, May 1993

Manufacturing and service companies that become world-class do so because they concentrate their efforts on different issues relative to average companies. Their performance criteria are different, and so are the contents of their management information systems. This article discusses the concepts and features that are needed for a management information system to support a world-class company.

The current status of management information

Currently the information available to management often makes the task of managing equivalent to 'flying blind'. Executives have to rely on 'gut-feel' rather than informed insight. The primary way to obtain valuable and useful information is 'management by walking around' – developing informal information by observation and discussion. Much time is spent 'fire-fighting' problems – attacking the symptoms rather than eliminating the causes.

A quantum leap will be required to implement a world-class MIS which provides an instrument panel of timely, relevant, and accurate information by which to manage the strategic direction and operations of the business.

Objectives of a world-class MIS

The objective of a world-class MIS is to assemble and present, in a timely manner, information which provides insight into the business to enable strategies to be implemented more efficiently and effectively so as to be able to influence the future performance of the business to fulfil its mission.

The mission statement should specify the basis on which the company wants to compete, be it product leadership, operational excellence, or customer intimacy (Treacy and Wiersema, 1993), the markets it wants to compete in, and how it wants to be perceived by its stakeholders. The formal, structured part of the MIS should enable all decision makers to monitor their progress in these perspectives of the business.

The role of information in a world-class company

Managers seek information that is timely, relevant, and accurate. It is unlikely that they will cease to develop and enhance their own abilities to observe and to gather information from their contacts irrespective of how good the formal information system becomes. The formal system plays a confirmatory and focusing role. Managers are reassured when there is consistency among information received from different sources. The formal information system should help increase the confidence in information by reporting within appropriate time frames (McKinnon and Bruns, 1992). The selection of the information to be included in the formal information system, and requiring explanations of these amounts, enables management to focus employees' attention on the matters deserving attention. The role of the formal information systems is:

- to provide non-financial performance information within time frames appropriate for action,
- to provide management reports containing financial and non-financial information as the basis for managerial learning about how day-to-day operations support the pursuit of corporate goals, and
- to provide financial reports as a basis for evaluating financial success and making comparisons with other companies in the industry.

The design of the MIS to support new management approaches

World-class companies have adopted a variety of new approaches to management which need to be included in the design of the MIS. These new approaches include:

Process management

Process management enables process redesign to achieve significant improvements in competitive capability. The focus will move from managing inputs to managing outputs. Activity-based management, as illustrated in Figure 1, will provide the structure for the information used to manage the business. The significant benefit of taking an activity-based management approach is that it combines cost management and performance management at the same place – namely, the activity.

However, for process management to really achieve its full potential, the management of the process has to be moved to the shop floor. This means that the collection and presentation of process management information has to be geared to the workers. Ingenuity is often needed to develop simple and unsophisticated information which gets to the heart of the management issues in the work area.

Figure 1: Activity-based management concepts

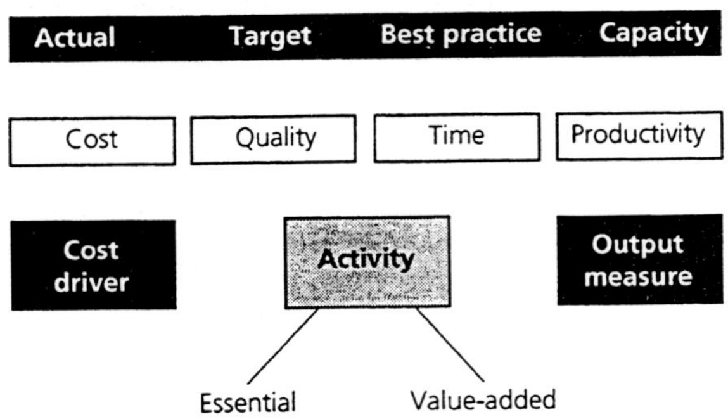

Capacity management

Almost all of what is referred to as overhead expenditure is committed in advance to provide the capacity of the infrastructure to do business (Cooper and Kaplan, 1992). The key to cost management in this environment is an understanding of how to assess surplus capacity, and how to eliminate it or use it effectively to produce new revenue.

Performance management

Most mission statements demand superior performance from the perspectives of many stakeholders such as customers, shareholders, and the community. This requires a move from purely financial performance measures to non-financial measures which will reflect the concerns of all the stakeholders identified in the mission statement. In addition, there are many non-financial performance measures which provide a better indicator of long term financial success than do traditional financial reports. Management need to define a business performance model which expresses their understanding of the relationship between action and results. A balanced scorecard of performance measures will include:

- operational measures of customer satisfaction and process performance,
- financial measures of past performance, and
- comparative information from the industry.

The capabilities and features of a world-class MIS

The primary role for a world-class MIS is to provide an integrated understanding of the financial and operational position of the organisation in a dynamic business environment. In order to play this role, the MIS should have the following characteristics:

- be flexible to change as the business does
- support the business strategies
- provide multiple views of the same data
- provide a balanced scorecard of financial and operational performance measures
- support a process view of the business
- provide for the fast collection and dissemination of data.

These characteristics are explained below.

Flexible

In a continuously changing business environment, the organisation needs to be able to change fast to respond to the market. The MIS needs to be dynamic – continuously changing to meet the needs of the organisation and continuously being improved. The attributes of the MIS which need to be able to change are not predictable, but include:

The organisation structure
An existing organisation structure is often a matter of preference, rather than necessity. As priorities and focuses change so will a change in organisation structure be required. The MIS should be able to model prospective changes and restate history on the reorganised basis.

Views of the business
Readily identifiable views of a business include a market view, a product view, a brand view. Flexibility requires the addition or removal of views from the MIS without a major restructuring of the database.

Performance dimensions
Although the performance dimension of most MISs is financial, there may be a need in the future to include dimensions such as quality, time, productivity, space or distance. Flexibility means being able to add or remove dimensions as needed.

Performance measures
The types of measures used to report on the performance dimensions also need to be flexible to allow a measure to be changed to another which is considered to be more representative of the underlying activity. For example, a measure of quality may be changed from the number of complaints to the time taken to complete a transaction which may be the underlying cause of the complaints.

Measurement bases
The MIS must cater for a number of measurement bases. Examples of measurement bases include actual, target, capacity, and best practice.

Support business strategies
The MIS needs to foster 'goal congruence', i.e. to ensure that the strategies and goals of the business cascade down to each level in the organisation in terms appropriate to each level. For example, achieving the consistent quality service might be measured in terms of market surveys for the executive level, but would need specific definition and measurement, for example, in terms of turn-around time or customer complaints, for a member of staff at the sales desk. In addition to its role in focusing the organisation, the MIS has an essential educational role. The selection of measures to be included in the MIS provides senior executives with the opportunity to coach subordinates on the issues that they consider critical to the success of the business.

Multiple views
Each event (internal or external) of economic significance to the organisation comprises a large number of data characteristics which provide information to the different audiences within the organisation. For example, a sale includes information of relevance to sales (who made the sale), marketing (the industry code for the use made or the product), distribution (the weight and size for transport scheduling), as well as finance (historical cost and replacement cost bases). The MIS must be able to report all these views in a synchronised manner. The MIS must be able to cope not only with predefined views as described above, but also with *ad hoc* requirements.

Balanced scorecard
A balanced scorecard (Kaplan and Norton, 1992) of financial and non-financial measures is needed to provide the best indicators of future financial performance of the organisation. It is not sufficient to measure sporadically such matters as the state of customer satisfaction, employee skills levels, and the organisation's contribution to the community. These matters need the same profile that the financial performance receives – what gets reported, gets attention.

Process management
Many manufacturing and service organisations are moving from a functional silo focus to a customer-oriented systems focus. This has been accomplished by using a process management approach which seeks to redesign the manner in which business is conducted in order to achieve significant efficiency improvements (Dilton-Hill and Glad, 1992).

Fast collection and dissemination of data
The need to provide non-financial performance information within time frames appropriate for action implies faster collection and dissemination of data. Faster collection requires the use of meters and measures that are contemporaneous with activity, or the use of human monitors who can input data as soon as the event has occurred. Faster dissemination requires electronic delivery in a format that is easy for managers to use. Unless the formal information system can operate at nearly the same speed as direct observation and informal reporting by managers and their subordinates, managers are not going to find the formal system supportive.

Key components of the MIS system
The key components of the MIS system are illustrated in Figure 2. The core of the MIS is a logically integrated 'event' database which includes all occurrences of economic significance to the organisation whether from client transactions (or summaries thereof) processed by the core business systems, from process management procedures, or from the external environment.

The events are recorded in their full richness to ensure that all functions within the organisation can draw the view of perspective that they require from the data in this system. The information requirements are driven from the 'top floor' to the 'shop floor' to ensure that the objectives of each level are aligned with the business strategies.

Figure 2: Key components of the MIS system

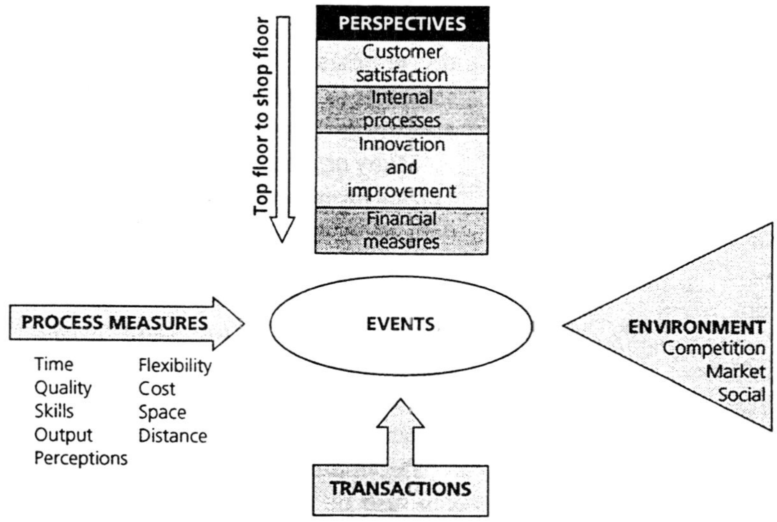

Conclusion

Changing into and remaining a world-class company involves a continuous process of change. Change is notoriously difficult to manage and sustain. In my opinion one of the major counter-forces to change is that the management information systems and performance measurement and reward systems are not revised in advance of change. Many companies try to manage change looking over their shoulders at the old information. Developing information to support a move to world-class often involves simplifying and eliminating much of the old financially based information, starting with data that may be simplistic and then implementing continuous improvement, moving from 'using the information you can get' to 'getting the information you can use '.

References

Cooper, Robin and Robert S. Kaplan, 'Activity-Based Systems: Measuring the Cost of Resource Usage', Accounting Horizons, *September 1992, pp. 1-13*

Dilton-Hill, Kevin G, and Ernest Glad, 'Business Process Management', Accountancy SA, *October 1992 pp. 317-322 and November 1992 pp. 355-359 and p. 362*

Kaplan, Robert S, and David P. Norton, 'The Balanced Scorecard – Measures That Drive Performance', Harvard Business Review, *January-February 1992, pp. 71-79*

McKinnon, Sharon M. and William J Bruns, Jr., The Information Mosaic *(Boston: The Harvard Business School Press, 1992)*

Treacy, Michael and Fred Wiersema, 'Customer Intimacy and Other Value Disciplines' Harvard Business Review, *January-February 1993, pp. 84-93.*

3.3 DATA WAREHOUSING

Data warehouses always appear to be something of a misnamed product. There is the expectation that a data warehouse is like a massive executive information system: all the trend information, detail about the organisation's products, recommendations for future output levels etc. will be found in the warehouse. However, this is not really the case: the data warehouse is really a much more humble tool, being literally a collection of data.

Basic information theory provides the idea that information is made up from individual items of data. The pieces of data, by themselves, are not particularly useful, but when processed in some way they become information, which is useful for decision-making. A data warehouse is simply that, a collection of data with very little 'use' for decision-makers. It is only when that data is processed in some way that useful information appears. So the name 'data warehouse' is correct – the warehouse does not provide solutions to problems, it simply provides the framework or data that can be used to find answers to those problems.

Many organisations are establishing data warehouses and then 'mining' those warehouses for important information about the business. This becomes possible because data entering the warehouse is 'normalised' or placed in a common format with data already in the warehouse itself. Data from many different parts of an organisation can therefore be added together to give a much broader view of the organisation. Sales to a common customer from many divisions in an organisation could, for example, be added together to give a total picture of the sales to that customer. The warehouse will then provide the means to extract this valuable information which would previously have been unavailable.

Depending on the available memory size of the warehouse, historical or legacy data can also be archived. This data can be accessed later to produce detailed historical analyses that again would not be available if the data were trapped in older computer systems. In information theory terms, it is probably better to think of the data warehouse as a 'database of databases'. It contains a vast amount of data relating to the organisation, and allows easy access to this data so that users can obtain the information they require. The overall aim is to find new relationships in the data that would not be evident if individual databases were maintained, e.g. total sales figure for one customer.

In the next article, Rod Newing presents an informative, and very detailed, analysis of data warehousing. It is highly recommended as an introduction to the subject although it does at the same time provide some background technical detail along with ideas for relevant computer applications that can be used in warehousing.

DATA WAREHOUSING
Rod Newing, *Management Accounting,* March 1996

At its simplest a data warehouse is a separate database of transactions dedicated to management information and decision support. Whereas the concepts apply to all organisations, the costs and benefits currently restrict the use of a data warehouse to large organisations with high volumes of data. It especially applies to organisations using mainframe systems for high volume transaction processing, although the principles are equally valid for smaller organisations.

A data warehouse is an architecture, not a product, and no single piece of software or vendor can provide all the components. It involves taking data from transaction systems, integrating it and storing it in a separate database where it can be accessed by users throughout an organisation for management information and decision support. It is not necessarily a single database but includes subsets of data distributed to local, departmental or workgroup servers.

The objective of a data warehouse is to give professional analysts and decision-makers the data they need to run the business. It is driven entirely by the information needs of the users and many organisations already use an Enterprise Information System to deliver summarised information from a variety of sources to managers.

The need for a data warehouse has arisen from increased competitiveness and the demand for more detailed information. A data warehouse provides an accessible store of transactional data for analysis using a variety of tools, including an EIS.

considerable technical problems. Data may be in a lengthy sequential file, which was designed for transactional processing not querying, so the query could conflict with the operation of the application and slow it down.

When the data is transferred to the data warehouse, it is translated into a common format and integrated. This means that related data from different sources is combined and merged. For instance, different transactions from the same customer from different systems will be combined to provide a fuller record of the customer relationships.

An example might be life assurance, pensions, domestic insurance, healthcare and automobile policies being issued from separate systems in a financial services company. This integration is a critical aspect of a data warehouse architecture. It allows organisations to assemble their entire relationship with a customer from different sources.

The database software itself operates in a client/server architecture. It is usually one of the established relational databases, which are also used for transaction processing, such as, Informix, Ingres, Oracle, Sybase or Teradata. Another major product is Red Brick Warehouse, which is designed specifically for decision support and claims a considerable performance advantage.

In order to provide acceptable performance from the large sizes of database which are created in a warehouse, powerful servers are required. These are usually parallel processing servers which utilise multiple processors to speed querying. These are specialist servers produced by companies like AT&T GIS, IBM, JCL, Pyramid, Sequent, Silicon Graphics, Sun, Tandem and Unisys.

Users have a wide range of options for working with data in the warehouse. Enterprise information systems (EIS), such as Forest and Trees, Holos Lightship, Metacube or Show Business can operate directly on the data in a relational data mart. Online analytical processing (OLAP) servers, such as Essbase, TM/I or LightshipServer, transfer the data to a separate multi-dimensional database for accounts using a spreadsheet link, Visual Basic or PowerBuilder. Products like Commander OLAP, Express, Powerplay or SAS combine an EIS with an OLAP.

Alternatively, they can be end-user applications, such as data access and retrieval tools (DART) or query tools, such as Brio, Business Objects or Impromptu. Professional tools can also be used, which require support from IT professionals but which can operate on the main central database in the warehouse. These include statistical analysis tools, such as SPSS, neural networks and various data mining tools. Other specialist software is also coming into use, involving data visualisation, intelligent agents and desktop mapping, such as MapInfo.

Although most of these tools can be used to access the data directly from the source applications, the data warehouse provides the ideal foundation. The data is already available and mapped and the promise of metadata integration will simplify the process of linking these applications with the data.

As users work with local data to analyse it, they create consolidations, trend analyses, what ifs or goal seek, thereby creating more data. However, these cannot be stored for further use and reference in the transaction database. The data warehouse provides a suitable location to save this data, where it can be accessed and shared, rather than leaving it on a local hard disk or on a file server.

Another problem of data availability is that historical data from legacy systems is often archived and therefore not available for decision support, other than as paper reports or spreadsheets. This problem is solved by migrating to a data warehouse architecture.

The information to be transferred to the data warehouse has to be defined in an information model. This represents the organisation's business and processes and involves defining the entities which the organisation needs to hold information about and the relationships between them.

The information model is used to create metadata, or a database containing 'information about information'. It should give status information, such as when the information was created or last updated, the update frequency, how it was derived and who is responsible for it. Two organisations, the Metadata Council and the Metadata Coalition have recently been set up to allow this metadata to be shared with feeder applications, warehouse management software and data access tools.

Data warehouse architectures place the data where it makes most sense from a business perspective. A data warehouse usually includes a number of smaller warehouses, often called 'data marts', which contain summary level information. It is cheaper, faster and easier to get departmental data from a dedicated departmental server than it is from the enterprise server.

The source of this departmental information should be the data warehouse, of course. The departmental server may be either the same relational database or an OIAP or EIS multi-dimensional database. There may be few direct users of the data warehouse and they may be mostly information professionals.

It is advisable to build a pilot data warehouse application first. This involves taking a small but significant part of the information needs of an important area in the organisation. The prototype should be small enough to be built, yet large enough to be meaningful. When the information needs have been established, a small sub-set of the final application is constructed and given to users.

One of the important outcomes of the pilot is that by using it data users will be better able to identify the benefits which a data warehouse can bring. This will enable a full cost benefit statement to be drawn up to continue migration to a data warehouse architecture.

Design, development and population of the data warehouse should continue a step at a time, in an evolutionary, not revolutionary manner. Whereas the prototype should take three months, the initial implementation of a data warehouse could take several years to complete. The eventual database sizes can be very large. Financial institutions can have a data warehouse which occupies up to two terabytes of disk space.

Data may well be incomplete or even absent or the same data may be available from different sources. However, the same data can exist in different places under different names or different data can have the same name in different places. Building the data transfer, integration and condensation routines are the major task in building the warehouse. Organisations like Carlton, CCA, Information Builders and Prism provide specialist software tools to manage the loading and administration of data in a warehouse.

Autonomous operating units may have local data warehouses fed by their own transactional systems. They contain data of interest only at the local level. The operating unit will need to map the relevant data onto the enterprise data structures in a local staging database, in order to incorporate it into the enterprise data warehouse.

'The success of a data warehouse project depends on its ability to encompass the real information needs of the business', says Pam Pipe, from Information Builders. 'Information needs must be identified in such a way that frequency of use can be established using metering software. Information which is only needed occasionally should be left in its original application to minimise the cost of setting up and maintaining the warehouse.'

The data warehouse can also be used to integrate external data into the organisation. This could include market research, demographic data, economic or market forecasts, research reports, competitor information, industry trends etc.

The benefits to a particular organisation of implementing a data warehouse architecture are unknown and cannot be established in advance. When the first prototype portion of the warehouse has been completed users start to identify the potential of decision support based on the warehouse. Fortunately the prototype can usually be produced quickly and cheaply.

Giving access to heterogeneous data across multi-vendor systems through a data warehouse architecture brings about a number of potential benefits. It can bring improved performance and efficiency through easier access to information, resulting in higher productivity and lower costs. It allows decisions to be made on the basis of more accurate and timely information and simpler information systems can result in less administrative support cost.

Many organisations increase business opportunities by reacting quickly to changing market conditions. They can enhance their ability to execute targeted marketing programmes, as well as measuring their effectiveness. The retailing, banking and financial services sectors have a compelling need to improve customer relationships.

They use data warehouses to integrate customer transactions in order to understand customers' buying profiles better. They then use this information to find new customers, retain existing ones and improve customer service. They have the high volumes of data, legacy applications and highly competitive marketplaces which enable them to justify the high costs of a data warehouse.

By retaining and analysing historical data and correlating cross-functional trends, a data warehouse provides a framework to develop an integrated view of the business activities. The information model will form the basis of designing new applications as the organisation grows. This will allow faster and more efficient implementation of new information systems. Lastly, by putting corporate data in centrally administered data stores, security, integrity, availability, recovery and optimum performance can be assured.

The data warehouse has acquired an unfair reputation, a product of marketing hype, mainly because it is the large-scale applications, requiring a massive investment in hardware and software, which have gained the publicity. MetaView is a new product which is being brought over by K2 Systems, the major accounting systems supplier. It is being launched at an introductory price which could provide a system for under £30,000.

There is a strong case for the introduction of a data warehouse architectures in a wider range of organisations and the cost can only decrease as more companies enter the market and competition gets more intense This will he good news for management accountants.

3.4 WE'VE GOT THE INFORMATION SOMEWHERE, BUT ...

The previous article on data warehousing concentrated on the theory and the computer applications that are used to establish a data warehouse. This second article on data warehousing starts to look at some of the practical applications of the subject. Although there is some duplication of knowledge, the article is included here for the examples of how supermarkets and other organisations are using a warehouse to try to enhance their business. These practical examples will be particularly useful in finding out exactly what is possible with data warehouses.

WE'VE GOT THE INFORMATION SOMEWHERE, BUT ...

Geoff Tyler, *Management Accounting*, June 1997

Directors and managers have a knack of asking for information which exists, but can only be extracted from the organisation's various systems by interrupting a lot of other, important, operational work. The response is all too often that the important work is interrupted because those trying to get it done do not have the power to hire and fire management accountants and the person wanting the answers does.

Today's computer systems and networks running order-processing, invoicing, production control, delivery scheduling, sales performances and so on certainly hold most if not all of the information even the most scientific of boards could need about the organisation. The problem is getting at it and doing so using an interrogation technique which can accept loosely defined terms of reference to allow for the unexpected.

The operational systems themselves are structured not to stop and provide us with snapshots of how they are doing, but to get on with the job in hand. It is not so much the extraction of raw data from these systems which causes delays—basic management reports are already a by-product of most such systems—but the processing and collation of the raw data to present meaningful analyses from which management can see obvious decisions. There is also the limitation that reports produced from an operational system can contain answers applicable only to that system. Hence a sales forecast will not take into account imminent raw materials shortages.

This is the situation data warehousing is marketed as addressing. A data warehouse is essentially a database configured for no other purpose than to receive data, be interrogated, sift through its files and produce the answers. It is separate from the systems from which the raw data is extracted. That extraction of data may be done overnight, say, when the systems are idle or at least at a low ebb, or it may be done more frequently, in background.

According to Ben Barnes, IBM's general manager of decision support solutions, 'Warehousing allows businesses to store information in a way that is accessible and understandable to non-technical decision-makers. Techniques such as data-scrubbing ensure the validity and accuracy of data entering the warehouse and, using various report-writing and query tools, critical information can be extracted.'

We shall return to query tools later but we must first, as end-users, pat ourselves on the back. Forms of data warehousing—transferring statistics to a separate database for analysis at leisure—have been in use since long before a systems egg-head coined the term to market a software package. Every company with a management reporting system which is more than a by-product of the operational systems—even though the two may be on the same computer or server—is practising data warehousing of a sort. The information technology industry did not invent data warehousing, rather it produced software products designed expressly to satisfy this need for which we had until then been using expedients.

What data warehousing has also done is focus attention on the best ways of extracting and storing operational systems' raw data such that it can be converted into useful information of which management may ask any questions of the *Why?*, *What cost?*, *What if?* and *How is?* variety and get fully researched answers.

That comment 'fully researched' is the crux of data warehousing design. 'A good data warehouse', suggests Roger Gilheaney, business development director of Cognos, 'will allow someone to ask challenging and sometimes non-specific questions like *Why is product line X selling well in Germany and not here?* The reasons may lie in design, customer preference, sales people's abilities and many other areas which the data warehouse may need to research to discover its clues and develop them into answers.

'Operational systems have far more information and answers, in the above sense, than we are ever able or, until now, have required to extract from them. Data warehousing provides this facility and, because it uses data drawn from systems which may not themselves directly interact, it can allow us to draw conclusions which are simply not possible using the operational systems alone.'

The technique warehouses use for this work is data mining. Barnes: 'Data mining takes warehousing goals further by allowing businesses to explore the data for previously unknown patterns, trends and associations. With data-mining technology, organisations can effectively leverage the enormous amounts of data they have compiled on customers, suppliers, industry trends etc., in order to make better-informed business decisions. We had a large chain of discount stores mine the information in its data warehouses to test the effectiveness of its advertising and merchandising practices. The result was higher sales for all products. A leading healthcare provider was able to target fraud and abuse in the form of inappropriate use of medical tests and services, unnecessary prescriptions and referrals.'

Data mining goes further than the existing query tools, OLAP servers and similar devices aimed at examining data. Those will not discover the hidden patterns and precedents. Data mining helps discover these by using algorithms capable of studying enormous quantities of intricate data and extracting that which reveals a relevance, to arrive at the eventual comparisons and explanations.

Users of conventional query tools need to know what answers they are looking for in what types of data – they have to establish a hypothesis. Data mining allows the user to raise queries without knowing what is in the database and therefore without preconceived ideas whence the solution may come. Nor need the user know what relationships will be found between areas of information hitherto assumed not to be related at all – though the user will normally need to specify the broad areas to be investigated by the mining operation.

There are limits – artificial intelligence, in the colloquial sense, is not too strong a term to apply to data mining but it is not neural, it will not draw intelligent conclusions from the information it presents. For example, data mining may attribute cost overruns on a project to materials wastage but it will not decide for itself to study the results of raw materials quality controls.

To get the benefits of data mining, data warehousing should not be implemented simply to fix one gap in the business knowledge. That will limit its capabilities to that area and will not take account of outside events which may influence it. An easy example is the common cross-reference – data warehousing or not – between accounts' customer payment records and sales' chase for new business. Spending time with known bad payers may be a waste that can be avoided – but the sales statistics alone will not reveal it.

Equally important, implementing data warehousing on a catch-all basis can overwhelm the intended application. The warehouse will be so full of immaterial data that it will become cumbersome. Gilheaney says the 20/80 rule applies – 20 per cent of raw data delivers 80 per cent of the required answers. The trick is discovering, during the planning process, which 20 per cent.

Supermarket retailers make interesting examples because of the huge amount of data they have on their equally huge product ranges. Safeway went with IBM's DB2 system for a data warehouse which would be flexible enough to grow. The store group's IT director Mike Winch said at the time, 'You don't want to have to start all over again whenever you make any major changes. The DB2 system means that regional variations in sales can be quickly spotted as well as other factors – the opening of a rival superstore nearby or special offers in local press promotions.

'For example, we sell 200 different types of cheese and considered dropping those products whose sales were low. But a close analysis showed that some of the cheeses that figured low on the overall list were usually bought by the top spenders. That kind of information helps us to make the right marketing decisions.'

Safeway started with non-critical systems such as marketing support to gain data warehousing and mining experience. Then came financial systems and business information such as Winch describes.

Deciding on the natural segments to which data warehousing can be applied and implementing them in a manageable way is the advice from Gilheaney. 'It is easier to add to the coverage and capability of the project as it begins producing results than to get it all right first time. The system should not be restricted as to the unexpected data relationships it can discover but it does need to be manageable.'

A data warehouse implemented as a series of, originally independent, data marts can interconnect those marts as it grows to give organisation-wide effectiveness.

Planning and implementation, then, are the vital steps as in all things. Gilheaney advocates a close working relationship. 'The user must decide, with some prompting perhaps, how the organisation has to move forward and from that a pilot scheme can be produced. Disciplines like ensuring the cleanliness of extracted data, correcting incorrect entries and so on are disciplines with which we can help, as are the links between the data warehouse and the operational systems. Those links need to interpret dissimilar data sources into a single form for the data warehouse.'

Dry-run testing of a new data-warehousing/data-mining project is essential. It could be done in-house, of course, but even that means some commitment to hardware configurations which may prove unsuitable.

The big players in data warehousing can provide their own test-bed facilities – though with sales strings attached, of course. IBM calls its version the Teraplex Complex, capable of testing live customer systems on a combined storage capacity of 12 terabytes.

Research by Cognos and Vmark found that 67 per cent of executives, including 60 per cent of IT specialists and 75 per cent of end-users, admitted to a relatively limited knowledge of data warehousing. Only 6 per cent of IT specialists claimed an extensive knowledge and 2 per cent did not even know if they had a data warehouse system.

The main reasons from IT specialists for not introducing data warehousing was lack of demand from the business generally – but in the same survey, end users disagreed and 40 per cent wanted to know why they had not had one implemented.

Data warehousing, of course, will only be as useful as those end-users make it. Dr Greg Bohlen at Benchmark Research found that training was by far the biggest headache for those who had implemented data warehousing: 59 per cent cited this ahead of cost of implementation, input data quality and meeting management expectations as their major challenges.

Gilheaney agrees: 'These findings are totally in line with our experiences in industry. Data warehousing is as much about company culture as technological change.... Without end-user need to gain knowledge from the data warehouse, the warehouse becomes redundant.'

According to Barnes, 'Early adopters of business intelligence systems (data warehousing and mining enveloped) are reporting returns on investment of six-to-one in 18 months. It's the best payback anyone can get with technology. Using conventional systems, industry analysts estimate that businesses currently analyse less than 7 per cent of in-house data.'

3.5 EXECUTIVE INFORMATION SYSTEMS: NOT JUST FOR EXECUTIVES ANY MORE!

Many organisations will have a variety of systems to provide information to different levels of management. These information systems will normally be split according to the management level that is receiving and using the information. This approach is providing managers with information appropriate to their level of control within the organisation.

Transaction processing systems are normally very good at supplying information about the individual day-to-day transactions and processes that have taken place in an organisation. This very detailed data is used by the operational managers in an organisation to control the daily activities of the organisation. Examples of the data produced would include items like units of goods manufactured, individual sales and purchases made and stock balances updated in real-time.

At the other end of the information scale the senior or strategic management need information that will help them understand how the business as a whole is performing. The information that is required at this management level would be highly summarised so an overview of the organisation is given. The usual delivery mechanism for this strategic information will be some form of executive information system. The EIS will effectively summarise information being produced by the organisation's TPS, as well as receiving other inputs like market and competitor data, and then present the resulting information to the senior management in some user-friendly format. Using this information, senior managers can make strategic decisions about the direction of the organisation such as amendments to product lines or even investment in new plant and machinery.

The next article by Messina and Singh is effectively querying this split in the information provision within the organisation. Rather than providing different information systems for different levels of management, the question is asked whether the different management levels should not have access to a common information system. In particular, providing access to the EIS by lower levels of management may well have some motivational effect on these managers. Not only would more junior management obtain a better picture of the organisation's activities, but they may also be able to do their jobs better because decisions could be related to the organisation as a whole, and not the specific operational area they are working in.

The first half of this article examines uses of an EIS, investigating in particular the information that an EIS can provide and how this can support management at all levels in an organisation. The second part of the article examines some EIS products and shows the benefits of using them in a case study drawn from an organisation based in California.

EXECUTIVE INFORMATION SYSTEMS: NOT JUST FOR EXECUTIVES ANY MORE!
Frank M Messina and Sanjay Singh, *Management Accounting,* July 1995

Management in Corporate America increasingly is using specialised computer-based systems on personal computers to aid in the decision-making process. These systems have come to be known as executive information systems (EISs), often referred to as executive support systems or enterprise information systems. Despite the nomenclature, these systems enable employees, as well as top executives, to gain access to the information needed to make decisions.

Until the advent of PCs, the use of computer technology by many executives was almost negligible because of the lack of technology to support the nature of executive work. The development of EISs was a direct response to the need for systems that could and would be used easily by senior-level executives. The main motivation was to develop a user-friendly environment so executives could tap into the existing wealth of corporate information (e.g. financial and operational performance data) that they need for decision-making. Both internal and external data would have to be incorporated into the system, but this needed information was difficult, if not impossible, to access. Quite often, the internal information was scattered throughout the organisation, residing on incompatible databases, while the external data simple were not publicly available as there was no mechanism to collect such information. Current information regarding an organisation's critical success factors could take days, if not weeks, to access.

Software vendors soon realised that if executives could be provided quick, easy access to this much-needed information, the vendors would have a captive market. Vendors of EIS technology created a 'push demand' by providing systems that executives could use easily. It was complemented by the 'pull demand' of executives who needed better information and were increasingly aware of the potential of information technology to help provide a strategic advantage. The result has been a market for EIS software that is expected to exceed $180 million by the end of 1995. Larger companies such as Georgia Power and Conoco have developed their own EISs, but with more software vendors entering the market, even the smallest of companies are able to afford their own EIS. In fact, most EIS software is surprisingly affordable and could pay for itself with time savings and access to better information.

EIS throughout the organisation

As a result of the increasing use of computer technology by senior executives, EIS has spread throughout the organisation. David Friend, CEO and founder of Pilot Software, a leading EIS vendor, labels EIS 'Everybody's Information System'. Information users at all levels of the organisation have realised that access to corporate information to aid in the decision-making process has become fast and easy. For example, Conoco, a major international energy company and a subsidiary of DuPont, began experimenting with EISs in the early 1980s. Currently, the EIS is used not only by senior managers but also by more than 4,000 other employees located in Houston, Texas, and throughout the world.

What exactly can an EIS do? An EIS:

- can provide on-line status access, trend analysis, exception reporting and retrieval of detailed lower-level data (drill-down);
- can extract, filter, compress and track critical data;
- can access and integrate a broad range of internal and external data;
- is user-friendly, requiring minimal training to use; and
- can present graphical, tabular and/or textual information.

Table 1 Support for motivating factors
Scale: 1 (not supported) – 7 (fully supported)

Motivations	Average (n=74)
Provide timely and faster access to information	5.75
Extract and integrate data from different sources	5.40
Monitor organisational performance	5.33
Provide information on critical success factors	5.32
Improve inter-organisational communication	5.28
Improve effectiveness of senior executives	4.97
Increase responsiveness to customer satisfaction	4.72
Improve organisational planning	4.53
Need competitive information	4.48
Improve quality of goods and services	4.43
Increase span of managerial control	4.42
Assist in cost-cutting measures	4.22
Assist in team-building	3.93

In addition, capabilities for electronic communication, financial modelling and *ad hoc* querying are standard features in most comprehensive EIS software packages. These attributes indicate that the main objective of an EIS is to present readily accessible and meaningful information to aid any and all users in the decision-making process. According to the results of our survey of 74 firms (banking/financial, manufacturing, governmental) using an EIS, the factors displayed in Table 1 were the main motivations behind developing and implementing an EIS.

An EIS is used primarily for assimilating, analysing and disseminating hard internal and external information (e.g. managerial, cost and financial accounting data) in a timely fashion. It not only reduces information float (the time that passes between asking a question and getting the answer), but it allows executives and managers to shape this information for strategic advantage. Timely and accurate *internal* cost information may be needed for planning (long- and short-term), pricing, product productivity, process efficiency and personal performance. For *external* data, EISs can be linked to public databases such as the Dow/Jones News retrieval and State Department releases. With more and more external data coming into database systems, the EIS will be able to incorporate much more timely external information.

Management accounting and EISs

Controllers, treasurers and even accounting managers should become the driving force behind EIS development, selection and implementation in their departments because they are the true data gatherers of the organisation. Their fundamental background in transaction processing systems and experience with accounting forms and reports will aid in determining the types of accounting-based information needed by executives and managers. David Friend notes that controllers can use EISs to provide better service to their customers. In fact, the largest number of users (25 per cent) of EISs in our survey indicated that accounting/finance was their primary area of work experience.

Because many of the data needed for long-range and even short-range decision-making often are considered confidential, appropriate controls are critical in an EIS. Accountants' keen knowledge of preventive, corrective, and detective controls should provide valuable assistance in developing and implementing an EIS.

One example of cost- and accounting-based information produced by an EIS may include data on measuring productivity, such as how increases in unit labour costs have been responsible for increases in a particular product's unit costs and have sparked increases in the product's selling price, which may have damaged the company's ability to compete in the market-place. An EIS allows comparison of current sales figures with industry trends to help project changes in market share based on changes in the selling price of a particular product. It lets a company compare its accounting-based data with competitors' data so it can justify increasing or decreasing product lines or even closing down an unproductive plant. Table 2 presents the support for various cost and management accounting needs as found in our survey.

Table 2 Support for cost and management accounting activities
Scale: 1 (not supported) – 7 (fully supported)

Activities	Average (n=74)
Extract and integrate data from different sources	5.42
Access consolidated financial and operational data	5.30
Provide information on critical success factors	5.22
Facilitate comparison of actual and intended results	4.98
Access detailed financial and operational data	4.78
Facilitate responsiveness/accountability of managers	4.55
Provide explanation for variance in results	4.22
Budgeting process	3.67

An EIS solution

The uses of accounting-based data for decision-making include the areas of planning and reviewing costs, capital budgeting and management control. Many of the data for executives usually are in condensed form, while the data needed by lower-level managers are more detailed. This difference can present a major problem for most companies' information systems, particularly when downloading data from the mainframe to the PC. An EIS can alleviate this problem and allow for the drill-down of information on all accounts to the level of detail desired by the executive or manager.

Yet the process is much more complicated than most EIS developers realise. Often, as previously noted, the databases are incompatible or the data reside in different proprietary databases. Thus, it becomes extremely difficult for an organisation to penetrate the tangled maze of existing data sources and extract meaningful and timely information. Pipelines must be built into these different sources of data. This inability to access and analyse data easily and turn them into useful information makes 'data management' the number one problem in building and implementing an EIS.

Arbor Software Corporation of Sunnyvale, California, appears to have found a way around the downloading problem. The company markets on-line analytical processing (OLAP) database products for mission-critical analysis for actual and projected enterprise performance data. OLAP software allows for dynamic, multidimensional, what-if analysis. Such capabilities are not provided by current database software based on the relational model. Arbor's main product, Essbase Analysis Server (Essbase), is a multidimensional database that is extremely fast and efficient because of its ability to define the organisation's reporting structure in the database. Basically, Essbase allows the company to paint a picture of what it wants.

Essbase is commonly used by managers and analysts who need multiuser access to consolidated enterprise information, immediate response regardless of query complexity, ease of use with popular spreadsheets such as Excel and Lotus 1-2-3 as front-ends, and powerful multidimensional analysis of enterprise performance data. For example, Pepsi-Cola International's Latin American division states that by using Essbase they can access consolidated data from many sources, such as accounting systems, product sales, marketing expenses, invoicing systems, product pricing systems and a myriad of other files and spreadsheets. Some applications that can be performed by Essbase are budgeting, forecasting, strategic planning, internal management reporting, tax planning, currency conversions, cost accounting, product mix analysis, performance analysis, allocations and data consolidations.

EIS software is generally implemented at the mainframe and client/server level. The software originated in the mainframe arena as a logical progression to the many database and DSS (decision support system) products that existed. For example, Comshare, a leading vendor of EIS software (Commander EIS), has a very powerful multidimensional database product (System W) for such use. Execucom, vendor of IFPS, a leading DSS software, had an EIS product called Executive Edge (acquired by Comshare in the early 1990s and no longer marketed). On this platform, the data and the program are kept on the mainframe, where the data are massaged, and then displayed on the PCs, which work as nothing more than dumb terminals. The vendors take advantage of the graphical user interface and some processing of the information at the PC level.

With the popularity of the client/server architecture, many EIS vendors have started to offer their products for this platform. The core software resides on the server, with much of the processing of the information being done at the PC level. This type of client/server architecture provides a lot of flexibility in terms of expansion of the number of users, development of applications and management of the software. A leading vendor in this arena is Pilot Software with its product Lightship. Generally, EIS software at this level is sold on the basis of the number of sites and licences.

EIS vendors

A number of companies market EIS software. Some of them are listed below.

Software	Manufacturer	Address	Telephone
Business Intelligence Software	**SAS Institute Inc.**	SAS Circle, Box 8000, Cary, NC 27512.	(919) 677-8000
Commander EIS	**Comshare Inc.**	PO Box 1588, Ann Arbor MI 48106.	(313) 994-4800
EIS Toolkit	**Microstrategy Inc.**	One Christina Centre, Wilmington, DE 19801.	(302) 427-8800
Essbase	**Arbor Software Corporation**	1325 Chesapeake Terrace, Sunnyvale, CA 94089.	(800) 858-1666
Lightship	**Pilot Software**	40 Broad Street, Boston, MA 02109.	(617) 350-7035
Monarch	**DataWatch Inc.**	234 Ballardvale Street, Wilmington, MA 01887.	(508) 658-0040
On Track	**Hyperion**	777 Long Ridge Road, Stamford, CT 06902.	(203) 321-3500
Xecutive Pulse	**Megatrend Systems Inc.**	1104 North Boulder Highway, Suite 1033, Henderson, NV 89015.	(800) 704-0035

Irrespective of the mainframe or client/server platform, commercial EIS software does not present the data directly from the various organisational databases. Rather, the software has pipelines built into the various databases (e.g. dB2, Oracle, Sybase, Informix, Access, etc.) from which relevant information is downloaded into a proprietary database designed just for the EIS software. Then the data are manipulated further for presentation of the relevant information in an appropriate format.

EIS at work

At one large regional insurance company, the EIS system is set up on several workstations in one company location. The types of data provided by the EIS are financial, operational and accounting in nature. The main users of the system include the company's assistant vice-presidents and cost accounting managers.

The EIS is a cost analysis system that gives the managerial and cost accounting managers the ability to retrieve data quickly from the mainframe into various pre-established cost reports. This process used to take one and a half to two and a half weeks with the old system, but by using an OLAP database (Arbor Software's Essbase), the data can be retrieved into a spreadsheet program in seconds. This change was accomplished by the development of approximately 90 preformatted screens (spreadsheets) for the managers, which were designed by the program developer at the company. The EIS allows the managers to perform detailed analyses on every line by providing the opportunity to drill down to any of the five dimensional levels of accounts. Thus, managers can track budget versus expense items on all accounts down to the true source. Also the system helps support bid preparation. The EIS has given the cost accounting managers a new way of thinking about the cost accounting system itself and has positively changed their view of the information system.

The estimated benefits to this particular company include:

- Major time savings in the area of information float (amount of time between asking a question and getting the answer);
- Annual savings of the salary of one manager; and
- Improved decision-making.

The use of EISs in organisations such as this one provides a viable option for executives and managers as an aid in making sound decisions in the market-place. EISs can help get the right information to the right person in the right format at the right time. The bottom line is that the use of EISs greatly enhances and facilitates the decision-making process, which in turn results in significant cost savings to the organisation.

3.6 THE INTERNET – THE SWISS ARMY KNIFE OF BUSINESS TOOLS

The Internet seems to be an unusual beast at the moment. On the one hand, everybody is talking about it and there is a race to build the most attractive, dynamic and interesting Web sites possible. On the other hand, relatively few people use it on a day-to-day basis, and even more have not even accessed it. A newspaper report (*Guardian*, 23 October 1997) shows that only 11 per cent of people in the UK use the Internet regularly and that over half of all households do not have a computer. I have run introduction to computer courses for senior staff in organisations this year where it is fairly obvious from demonstrating the Internet that this is their first view of the Web. Knowledge of the Internet is still very limited.

An organisation making use of the Internet appears to have a very limited audience, at least from the point of view of trying to sell goods. But using the Internet as a sales tool only may be an unjustified approach. Perhaps the question to ask is what uses can organisations make of the Internet rather than simply assuming that the Internet is one vast electronic marketing device. This approach is justified if you look at what the Internet can actually do. The Internet provides, among other things:

- Communication via e-mail (and telephone if you have the right hardware and software);
- A quick and reliable courier service for documents;
- A market-place for organisations to publicise their products and services;
- Access to data on other organisations;

- A place for customers to place orders;
- Most importantly, savings in time and money due to the speed and ease of the communications system.

Jeremy Rasmussen discusses all of these points and more in this next article. Although the Internet is seen here as a Swiss army knife, providing many different tools in one application, there is one major issue that will still need to be addressed, that is, simply navigation of the Internet itself. Information overload may well be a problem here. Most employees will find two basic problems with Internet usage:

1. How do I find the information required?
2. Having obtained a list of possible sources of information, how do I select what is relevant?

Although the Internet does have some fairly powerful search engines, they will only give a list of possible information sources. There is still the issue of entering the correct words into the search in the first place to find the Web site that is needed. So if your organisation is called the Bavarian Balaclava Company, how do you differentiate yourself from the BBC? (Try looking for BBC.COM on the Web, you may be surprised!) Then, having found a list of relevant sites, do you really want to look at all the, say, 1,346 possible hits for the information you require? The point is that the Web is already large and organisations will have to take time to make sure that they are easily visible on the Web.

Anyway, have a look now at the potential benefits of using the Internet. Then, if you have not yet had a 'surf', have a go!

THE INTERNET – THE SWISS ARMY KNIFE OF BUSINESS TOOLS
Jeremy Rasmussen, *CMA Magazine*, March 1996

Some say the Internet is a fad. It is cumbersome, requires too much hardware and software. It offers no enhanced business value or quality of life. It can never replace conventional communication or media as we know it

Others are more sanguine. They believe that the Internet has reached its maturity, already achieving great change in the way people work, educate and communicate. But its system requirements, training demands and security needs limit its future.

The evidence shows, I believe, that the Internet is still in its infancy. It is evolving exponentially. Its future is being affected – but not shaped – by trial and error, software developments and businesses' sense of opportunity.

The early years of the Internet indicate where its future is headed because many of the forces are still at work.

The net originated with the U.S. military's Arpanet (Advanced Research Program Net) which linked the military, its contractors, and scientists working on military research. Arpanet was powerful but difficult to use. It demanded computer terminals and expertise that many managers and executives simply did not have. These two requirements gave power to those who had the knowledge and tools. Largely out of sight of their bosses, the engineers and scientists traded candid comments about the quality of research. They passed judgment on their managers and superior officers and created games to show off their computer skills. They also devised software to make their lives easier.

Some of the play and much of the work helped develop the current technology. The need for faster communications than modems (300 baud was state of the art until the early 80s, 14,400 is standard today) led to a search for digital forms like ISDN and ATM. Hard-to-manage networks gradually yielded to hardware designs and software. But most importantly, smart hackers wrote software that made the job of finding, managing and manipulating information much easier. They used digital technology to incorporate images, color and sound into their text-dominated world.

Arpanet was text-based. With the advent of the World Wide Web (WWW or the Web), the Internet has become a multimedia environment with graphics and sound that now runs the gamut from research to games, rock music to pornography and serious business communications. It is the business uses on which I want to focus to help explain why this phenomenon is still in its infancy.

Increasingly, firms transmit images, voice, video and data over the Internet. They use it for point-to-point communication between their own offices, their clients, and their suppliers. Estimates, technical drawings, software services, product information, and software upgrades are the stuff of these communications. A draft of this article was transmitted back and forth over the Internet so that it could be edited electronically.

To reach beyond the group of their clients and suppliers, many firms have Web pages for marketing and information. At least one firm posts all of its press releases about sales agreements on its Web site.

The daily press does not report the releases but the financial analysts who track the firm, which is publicly traded, read the releases avidly and the stock has risen.

Another firm has set up a job-posting service, charging other organisations for posting a vacancy on a Web page. The service appeals, particularly, to organisations looking for candidates with knowledge of the Internet.

Projected growth is huge

No single reason compels the growth of the Internet. But it is expanding asymptotically (see Figure 1).

Figure 1: Projected growth is huge

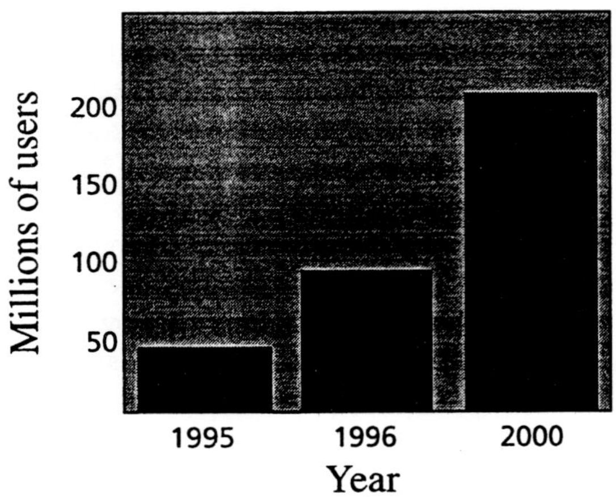

The Internet links 30 million computer users worldwide through thousands of smaller networks, all interconnected using a common communication protocol. Analysts expect 80 million Internet users by the close of 1996 and 200 million by 2000. (In addition about six million Americans now use services like America OnLine, CompuServe or Prodigy; and an estimated 3 5 million will subscribe by 2000.)

International Data Corp. (IDC) further predicts a growth in electronic commerce revenues to more than $200 billion by the year 2000. This indicates an enormous shift in business away from services like couriers, printed directories and catalogues, and print advertising driven, initially, by the cost savings and speed. It also reflects wealth creation, with organisations offering whole new services, such as the job postings, over the Internet.

As a form of communications, the Internet is growing faster than telephones, courier services, television or radio networks, and cellular networks because it offers different capabilities and, in some ways, more than these do. Admittedly the base is smaller, but the numbers are still impressive.

Business values

No single reason explains why firms connect to the Internet. This fact underlines its flexibility and power. Several factors appear to recur. As the examples below indicate, the Internet:

- Helps an organisation leverage the investment in its information systems.
- Saves money in marketing and delivery. Enhances productivity by eliminating steps.
- Strengthens the work environment by making important and relevant information available in a timely and useful way.
- Augments communications by bringing geographically dispersed project teams together in on-line discussion groups and document-sharing forums.

Flexibility and productivity

For many uses, the multimedia flexibility is preferable to a unidimensional fax, or voice-only phone lines. Sending machine drawings or plans by e-mail saves time. The advantages are more than speed, however. For example, someone may want to incorporate faxed information into a presentation or memorandum. To do so, they have to rekey the material. Files taken from the Internet can be used and modified according to the recipient's needs, quickly and without the errors that often occur when a document has to be rekeyed.

Another flexibility advantage of the Internet is that its learning curve is more like a series of small steps. A person can begin using the Internet for e-mail, or for information searches, and be productive in less than an hour. The same person can expand his or her knowledge in a series of small steps, learning the techniques at the time he or she needs them, in a meaningful context. One of the things that makes this easy is that much of the Internet is intuitive.

Time and money savings

Firms can extend their ability to service their clients through user group forums. Rather than sending a service representative to make a call, Cisco, the Internetworking provider, solves more than 90 per cent of its customer' concerns over the Internet, frequently using other customers in specific industries as resources. Many documents can be transmitted via the Internet instead of shipped by courier.

Distribution

An increasing number of firms are delivering software upgrades or 'fixes' over the Internet. The payoffs in customer satisfaction, speed, and simplicity are enormous. Organisations can also list the location, price, and availability of products for customers on a regularly updated basis, saving a prospective customer the hassle of having to phone around to various potential distributors or retailers.

Marketing

The Internet provides new marketing opportunities for firms to reach the users, who often fall outside the reach of traditional media. The demographics and sociographics of Internet users are attractive to many organisations, making the effort worthwhile.

- They are computer users, more comfortable with technology than non-users. They seek out ways to leverage technology. They have enough experience with learning curves and the rewards of perseverance that they stick to the technology until they master it. They are less likely to be moved by fantasy marketing than by technical specifications and knowledge of how a product performs.
- They use their computers to work at home and office, routinely using the Internet to connect to their office information resources. The people work longer hours because they can work at home, but they feel they have more control over when and where they work, so they mind it less. They also feel that they are more productive because they are exercising control over stresses like fatigue and competing schedules.
- They use their computers and network access for personal applications as well as business, whether shopping for cars or vacations, or getting news and stock market updates.
- While many Internet users have a higher mean income than non-users, they may also choose some alternative lifestyles. The Internet enables this choice. Some free-lance writers, for example, live and work far from their clients, in more bucolic settings than cities, and stay in touch over the Internet. One talented researcher, house-bound by acute arthritis, earns his living from his home over the Internet.
- They are well educated and tend to be more sceptical than non-users. 'Lifestyle' advertising, prominent in beer commercials, does not have the same appeal.
- They do not consume broadcast media as much as non-users. This arises, in part, from the longer work hours and in part from the value systems.
- Anti-authoritarianism characterises many of their communications. They see how fast they can work and make decisions when they cut across channels. Yet, they combine this streak with increased productivity for the firms in which they work.

Like many other car firms, Mercedes-Benz has a site on the Internet. It provides detailed information on the firm, its models of car, the technical specifications, the local dealerships, and the pricing. The firm does not picture its cars with models in glamorous settings but it does provide the basic information needed, including pictures.

Any size of firm can benefit from the Internet

Virtually any size of company can take advantage of the Internet. The real issues are strategic rather than financial or operational. For example, one multi-division firm had many 'low-grade' customer complaints. Customers would change the name of a contact person or the mailing address with one division but have to repeat the process with every division of a company because each system was independent. The issue was not whether technology could solve this problem, but whether the firm had the commitment to customers and the discipline to unify the databases. When the firm focused on the issue, it realised that it could achieve many other customer benefits through a disciplined customer focus and at the same time reduce its operational overheads. The Internet solutions, including a customer user group site, are the final steps in a complete rethinking of the firm's commitment to customers.

Firms, ranging from one office connected to a public network to corporations with tens of thousands of employees, use the Internet for enterprise applications. They use them to facilitate doing business with customers and suppliers; to enhance their public relations by having information available around the clock, worldwide; to leverage their organisation's resources, wherever they are located; to improve their customer support while reducing costs and to link their internal e-mail to the Internet; to put staff in touch with customers and suppliers around the world at a fraction of the telephone costs. The advantages of effectiveness and economy work for them just as well as for bigger firms.

Increasingly, internal, corporate 'intranets' provide the platform for communicating with one another, collaborating on projects or issues, and co-ordinating processes and workflow. The intranet provides a form of wide area network (WAN) that becomes the primary gateway for every business, professional, commercial on-line service and private networks such as GEIS, MHS, x.400, America OnLine and CompuServe.

Within firms, document-oriented information such as account management, travel expenses, applications for training courses, customer-service tracking or policy updates are a natural use of the Internet. Changes to the forms can be made at any time. The delays in communicating the material are minimised.

One firm uses its own internal Web page to provide new product and competitive marketing information and tips to its sales force across North America. In another firm, employees can use the Internet to check on the vacation days they have accumulated, rather than using staff time to check. The Internet also helps firms organise frequent interaction among busy, travelling workgroups.

One large organisation's marketing department keeps on schedule and in touch with its suppliers and each other, by using the Internet, even when the managers are on the road. The impacts are two-fold. Staying in touch is easier and faster. With more time to plan and consider material, and more inputs, the quality of work is better.

Finally, part of the power of the Internet is that supporting software permits users to combat information overload. It enables them to filter out news discussion groups, view documents at a later time and keep hot lists of important documents.

Customers share the benefits

Customer benefits from using the Internet mirror those of firms. People can access it whenever they want, for communications, research, placing orders, support and service. They are not restricted to office hours for phoning. The benefits they gain are that the Internet:

- Improves the quality of the suppliers' work by eliminating the need to transfer information from one form, such as a fax, to another.
- Improves the speed and access to information.
- Enables current information on pricing, availability and delivery, rather than a guess from an order taker.
- Makes firms easier to deal with by offering clients and suppliers access to product and service knowledge bases, order entry and status systems as well as sales, marketing and corporate communications information.

The Internet is a powerful tool, not a solution

The Internet is not a magic pill. There are other process and discipline issues involved. Staff can have all of their increased productivity soaked up by electronic junk mail if there are no guidelines on use. Security issues have to be addressed. If people make many small changes to documents rather than focusing on a comprehensive review of materials, then this lack of disciplined focus will eliminate the productivity gained by the technology. The technology alone will not provide improvements.

The Swiss army knife

The Swiss army knife is synonymous with multiple functionality. It can be a spoon, a nail file, scissors or screwdriver and more. The issue is not what it can do but how the user wants to use it. The Internet offers corporate users tremendous flexibility. It opens doors for new forms of marketing, delivery and services which can help an organisation achieve its objectives. These advantages, which are already here, will grow in the future as more users join the Internet, as more software firms develop ways of tapping the potential, and as more people move up the learning curve.

3.7 INTRA, NOT INTER!

One problem that has faced many organisations is simply sharing information between different departments, especially where those departments are using different systems from necessity. For example, a production department will be using some form of production scheduling software but the training department, which organises training for all employees, keeps training information on a Lotus Notes or similar application. Although it is unlikely that the training department will want to view production records, employees in production would like to see when and where they have been booked on to training courses. Unfortunately, neither department has the ability to use the other department's software, making communication difficult. The situation could be made worse by incompatible hardware or communications software, so telephone or written memos may be used to transfer information.

An easier communications method could be to use an Internet within the organisation, or an intranet to give it the correct title. The training department could set up a Web page containing details of all training courses for production staff. This could then be accessed via an internal Internet browser and course information obtained. Alternatively, the facility could be provided to allow the production staff to book their own training courses on the training department's own Web site! Using the intranet, therefore, allows communication to be made between different departments quickly and simply.

The above example may be fairly simplistic, but it does serve to show some of the potential benefits of using an intranet. All that is being done is to establish an Internet within an organisation. All the features and functionality of the Internet can be used although there will be no communication links outside the organisation.

Although intranets can be established to overcome problems of information sharing within an organisation, there appears to be no reason why the 'net' could not be expanded to allow third-party access or include other communication systems like electronic data interchange. In the next article, Alan Perkins takes a look at how intranets are starting to be used in an Australian organisation which will hopefully provide some useful food for thought on the use of intranets. A properly thought out and set up intranet would provide an excellent method of sharing information in many organisations. This system may well provide one of the most exciting developments of the next few years.

INTRA, NOT INTER!

Alan Perkins, *Australian Accountant*, November 1996

The media is full of references to the Internet but talk of intranets leaves many people perplexed. Yet an intranet can provide just as many, and perhaps more, opportunities for business than its better-known relative.

An intranet is a 'mini-Internet' – a network of computers set up to be closed to the outside world, allowing access to traditionally 'hard to get at' data to those within the organisation. Unlike traditional networking systems, an intranet is designed to run the same application types as on the Internet. These include e-mail and everything that encompasses the World Wide Web.

With animated instructions of how to sell a product or assemble it, pictures of all staff available, and voice memos concerning customers and suppliers, the technology has many attractions, including the support for hyperlinks. Hyperlinks enable links from one place in a document to another, or indeed to another document which may be on the same computer, a computer in another branch, or indeed in another country.

To the end-user, the location of the stored document is irrelevant. One moment, they may be looking at a picture of a spare part; with the click of a mouse on the picture, they may be looking at an instruction sheet explaining how to install it.

Opening up

Using an intranet as an information reference tool is important but the future holds a great deal more for this technology. With appropriate security measures. the intranet can be opened to the outside world. This will enable companies to provide access to their systems by their trading partners (or prospects) with a view to doing business

Such access could include stock inquiry, pictures and a description of a selected stock item, and pricing and availability information. Customers would be able to enquire about the status of their orders, or outstanding balances. Prospects would be able to find out information about the company, its major accounts and history. Customers could even place orders on the system.

Ultimately, a customer will be able to, from home or the office, visit a store and use a virtual reality system to 'walk' up and down the aisles, examine a product on the shelf, remove it to have a closer look at the packaging, the contents, the ingredients. and, if satisfied, drop it into a shopping basket.

This has many implications for Australian businesses. Customers of many boutique stores are already turning to the Internet for their purchases – why buy at a local store, if you can go to the source in America, Denmark or anywhere else and purchase, via computer, the product directly at a lower price and receive it within a week?

This is one of the challenges of change. However, change always brings opportunities for those prepared for it. The Internet offers the astute entrepreneur a potential customer base of many millions. For the Australian marketer, the Internet is a boon which removes the tyranny of distance. An Australian company, Sausage Software, is a case in point. Writing software tools for the Internet, Sausage Software's product Hog Dog sold $3000 in its first week of sales over the Internet; in the next month, sales were $36,000; the following month, they reached $52,000 Recently, sales had reached $469,000.

Information flow

Another – often underestimated – opportunity presented to an organisation is market research. Web crawlers are often more likely to respond to a survey about their opinion on all sorts of things thrust at them. With the number of hits many business sites get, there is a gold mine of marketing data waiting to be analysed.

To take advantage of all these opportunities a company needs to have in place good infrastructure designed to handle a potential world market. While costs of doing business over the Web are relatively small, a tightly integrated backbone is essential. The ultimate order handling system will work like EDI (electronic data interchange – a system used by corporates like Coles Myer to automatically place orders directly into the accounting systems of their suppliers). This means that when a customer places an order with a company, the accounting system should be able to take the order in as a sales order directly from the customer's entry so that there is no reprocessing. At present, no such system exists for small business, but at Business Manager Software we are working on such an addition to our Ambassador package for release in early 1997.

The intranet concept has other implications for business. Client-server database systems provide facilities for storing business events or triggers in the database. Using this with an intranet can mean that the accounting system can be automated to perform predefined tasks.

For example: a company has their head office in Sydney and a remote warehouse in Port Moresby. In Port Moresby, there are 120 widgets in stock and the database has been told to hold a minimum of 100 units and a maximum of 500. If someone places an order for 40 widgets, the database can e-mail the purchasing officer in Sydney, notifying them that the Port Moresby office is going to run short and requires another 420 units. The e-mail, which is automatically generated by the database, then asks the purchasing officer if they want the order placed with the supplier. If the response is 'yes', a purchase order is automatically raised with the supplier.

Setting up an intranet requires several pieces of equipment and software. At the workstation end, a company needs to have a Web browser system on each machine and an e-mail system. The Web browser is the window on the Web documents as 'pages'. Currently, the two major browsers battling for supremacy are Netscape Navigator by Netscape and Microsoft's Internet Explorer. Both are inexpensive, or even free. Both support Java, a programming language developed for the Internet. At this stage, only Internet Explorer supports Active X, a new technology developed to support some very useful technology in the Web pages. Active X will have a major part to play in Windows 97 and other Microsoft future products.

At the server end, an intranet server software product is required. The server should be a powerful computer running Unix or Windows NT. Expect to pay around Aus $20,000 or more to establish a fully fledged intranet for a company of approximately 50 employees. Certain business applications, such as providing integration to the accounting software, could be done in isolation.

Faster, faster

As the communications backbone gets faster and the cost of ISDN access comes down, we will see more and more use of the Internet as an integral part of the way businesses behave. New suburbs around Australia are being developed with homes being cabled into the infrastructure. The number of users throughout the world is growing at an incredible rate.

For many businesses, failing to plan for this eventuality may ultimately mean that they will have a lot of catching up to do. For those who plan to integrate this new feature into their current plans, opportunities may present themselves from a wide variety of sources.

For software developers like Business Manager Software, the burgeoning of computer-based communications technology provides challenges and opportunities to enable clients to move into a new way of doing business.

3.8 INTERNET CUSTOMER SERVICE

The final article in this section looks some of the ways that the Internet can be used to provide goods and services.

In previous articles, the idea of providing information internally within an organisation has been discussed. While this is a good idea, there is the issue of the best way of presenting the information and making it easily accessible to the users. This problem parallels the situation of firstly attracting a customer to a Web site and then trying to get that customer to navigate around the site and hopefully purchase something from it. Good Web site design is therefore essential to meet these objectives.

The reason for including this article is therefore to see how some organisations are approaching establishing or upgrading their Web sites. This will provide some relevant examples on how organisations can establish and maintain their own intranets. The four-point summary at the end of the article is especially relevant in this respect, with the need to focus on the customer (that is, the other departments within the company in an intranet situation) being the most important feature of establishing the site.

INTERNET CUSTOMER SERVICE
***Business Computer World*, September 1997**

Customer service has been the maxim of every efficient business for the past decade or so. But the message that looking after customers is the key to successful trading has been slow to arrive on the Internet.

Many businesses weighing up the pros and cons of trading over the Web have been preoccupied instead with bottom-line factors, assessing the Internet more for its potential to cut sales and distribution costs. Some see online business as a means of talking more directly to customers, but often in terms of collecting information about buying habits, or substituting a Web page for a telephone helpline as a way of providing information about the company.

So far, few companies have cottoned on to the notion that the Internet can be used to provide the kind of enhanced, personalised customer service that is the marketeer's dream. Even in theory it's not hard to see the possibilities. For instance, keeping track of both stated customer preferences and actual customer buying patterns on an individual basis could provide businesses with substantial marketing information.

Blackwell's Online Bookshop, for example, is building a system that it hopes will assist in compiling lists of appropriate titles for customers. So, if a customer has ordered, say, two books on roses, Blackwell's wants to be able to use its data on customer buying patterns to suggest books on pruning or ornamental water features as the next most likely purchases.

However, tuning systems to the needs of customers is not as easy as it seems, and this is one of the reasons it is not yet widespread. What's more, some services are more difficult than others to get right, such as ordering fresh food over the Internet – though that hasn't deterred most of the large supermarket chains from trying. Tesco is currently running trials in north London, and both Sainsbury's and Somerfield have pilot schemes. In the last two cases, though, it is notable that the trial customers are staff at technology companies – Hewlett Packard and IBM, respectively – who will be comfortable with the notion of online ordering.

There is, potentially, a greater problem than delivery and that is handling customers efficiently. Most companies' systems are tuned to the internal processes of the organisation, such as product or function, and it is difficult to turn the information needed by such processes into an easy-to-use, customer-focused system. In theory, a customer should need no more than their name and address to be able to deal with an organisation; in reality, they often need to remember complex information, such as customer reference numbers or product numbers – data demanded by the internal systems.

However, the flipside of this is that, because as consumers we've all become used to these cumbersome processes, it's relatively easy to provide a service that customers will see as a step up from average. That's certainly the view of Rob Bruce, marketing manager of Broadvision, whose One-to-One Web application is being used by Blackwell's and other customers, including the Spanish bank, Banco Santander, which has launched a customised Internet banking service. 'You don't need to do very complicated things to please customers a lot,' says Bruce. 'Customers like even quite simple things, because they've never had them before.'

Providing really good customer service over the Internet largely depends on intangibles, such as branding. But, for those companies that get it right, the opportunity to build up a close, profitable relationship with customers can be invaluable.

Indeed, regarding the Internet as a vast bargain basement could prove to be the undoing of many businesses. In online trading, just as in the regular kind, quality and customer service are likely to be the long-term differentiators.

Subject: Blackwell's Online Bookshop
Activities: selling books and periodicals
Installation: Broadvision's One-to-One
Uses: to run Blackwell's global online book and periodicals service

Blackwell's is usually thought of as a long-established university bookshop in Oxford but, since its foundation in 1879, its business has prospered from that base to the flourishing £500m group it is today.

In addition to its 80 retail bookshops, Blackwell's specialises in supplying a full range of academic, medical, legal and technical books and periodicals to libraries and individual customers around the world. Going online is a natural extension of this mail-order business for Blackwell's, which was early into the Internet market.

'Blackwell's was one of the first commercial organisations online in the UK, in 1989, and has been selling books online since June 1995,' comments Herbert Kim, head of marketing and sales at Blackwell's Online Bookshop. 'The Internet is a natural extension of our existing business and is seen as a way to serve a lot of Blackwell's customers abroad.'

Initially, says Kim, the online facility was regarded as an additional service for customers which needed relatively little investment from the group. But sales over the Internet have grown rapidly. 'With sales of £500,000 on an investment of virtually nothing, this is probably the most profitable return on any investment,' says Kim. 'So, this year, we have decided to invest a fair bit of money – more than £1 m – to make this a really first-class bookshop.'

One of the key aspects of the online service is the access it gives customers to Blackwell's database of books and periodicals This covers the 150,000 titles directly stored in the Oxford shop, but will now be expanded to 1.2 million titles, with full bibliographic data about each. 'We will be making it easier for customers to find books, by giving them quick and easy ways to search the database,' says Kim. 'But there's a lot more we can do as well. We can provide recommendations from Blackwell's highly experienced staff on specific titles and, because we are a global company, we can deliver anywhere in the world. This means we will have global reach but local delivery – that can't be done by an average bookshop on the Internet.'

Also important is the ability to personalise the relationship between Blackwell's and its customers. 'We chose the Broadvision engine because it offered the most flexibility,' says Kim. 'Blackwell's sales reps don't just sell books, they build up a profile of customer buying habits, and Broadvision will help in that mission by keeping track of buying and suggesting titles to customers. We believe this is the real cutting edge – the attempt to personalise the service back to the end-user.'

Subject: Arq Activities
Activities: developing online services for UK mail-order and catalogue companies
Installation: Web site based on Icat's electronic commerce system
Uses: entry point for mail-order and catalogue companies trying out online services

Developing good customer services over the Internet is sometimes a complex mix of online and traditional approaches, as Arq's experiences have proved.

Arq is a Bath-based company specialising in online services for UK mail-order and catalogue companies keen to dip a toe into Web-based trading without major up-front investment.

Its main project is the Catalogue Online UK (Couk) Web site, which provides mail-order and catalogue companies with a number of services. These include a directory, where companies can post their details for a six-monthly fee of £100. The directory provides leads to the companies and enables individuals to request specific product catalogues.

Arq is also setting up a department store on the Web site – due to go live in September – which will provide a cheap means for traders to advertise a selected number of products without making a major investment in Web technology. It will cost them £10 a month to sell each product in this way, with a minimum cost of £600 – 10 products for six months.

'The aim is to develop the 'everything' site for home shopping,' says William Pryor, Arq's managing director. 'The directory provides an easy way for catalogue companies to get their feet wet online and work through the fear and doubt of using online services, while the cost of being in the department store is small potatoes compared with the cost of printing even the cheapest paper catalogue.'

Arq's next stage in enticing traditional catalogue companies on to the Internet is to design a full bespoke online catalogue, which it has just done for tableware company Scott's of Stow (www.scottsofstow.co.uk). Here, too, customer service is of prime concern: while the product catalogue on the site is straightforward, Arq has included several features aimed at personalising the experience. Once users have registered on the site to buy something, the shopping-cart feature logs their purchase. This means that the system builds up a 'shopping profile' so that, on future occasions, it can suggest items or special offers based on previous purchases.

'In the US, sites making serious money are those that allow surfers to contribute a bit of themselves,' says Pryor. 'We want to work towards building sites based on communities.' The next Arq project is an official site for the City of Bath that will include shop details alongside the many attractions of the city. 'We want to put shops into their context. Sterile shopping malls are just that – sterile lists,' comments Pryor.

Subject: Banco Santander
Activities: banking
Installation: Banca Supernet Internet banking service, based on Broadvision One-to-One
Uses: providing personalised online banking

Banco Santander believes it will be the first bank in the world to offer its customers personalised online banking services. To help it achieve this it has installed Banca Supernet, an Internet banking service, which has been built with the Broadvision One-to-One application system on top of existing banking systems.

Santander is the leading financial group in Spain, with a net turnover last year of $951.7m, and it has major operations in the US and Latin America. Banca Supernet provides full branch service capabilities on the Internet, enabling users to access their accounts to conduct standard banking practices from their desktop as well as carrying out other transactions, such as transferring funds to other financial institutions.

In addition to its fully operational online service! Banca Supernet is customised to users' requirements. They can choose one of four different site 'styles' for the presentation of information, each defined by a different set of fonts, colours and style of the user. Within each of these styles, a further four options are available, enabling users to view first what they regard as most important, such as their credit card balance, or the performance of particular companies on the stock market.

Additional options are due to be added to the service, such as an alert that will let the user know, either by e-mail or phone. when something happens in their account, such as their balance dropping below $500.

Jorge Mata, head of multimedia banking at Banco Santander, says the single objective of the Internet banking service was to increase customer loyalty. And this is why the bank chose the Broadvision system, with its dynamic personalisation features that allowed the bank to tailor its services to customer needs.

One of the key components of Banco Santander's online initiative is a single point of service for customers. The bank's pledge is to answer e-mail from the Internet in less than 24 hours. Customer requests will be responded to either by e-mail or phone, depending on the request and the preferences of the customer.

Internet customer service lessons:

1. Focus on the customer: too many services concentrate on the seller's own processes, such as customer reference and product numbers.
2. You don't need to make things complicated to please customers – simple things can be very helpful, so go back to basics.
3. Keep processes straightforward – but bear in mind the complex way different customer communities may overlap.
4. Ensure there's a dialogue between yourself and your customers but, at the same time, keep a close track of real buying patterns – there's a difference between what customers say they do and what they actually do.

Chapter 4

Information and Employment

4.1 INTRODUCTION

So far this book has concentrated on information itself and the systems providing that information. This final section looks at the effect of changes in information and information systems on employment and the difficulty individuals can have in coping with large volumes of information.

The articles in this section are:

- 'Just press the button' – looks at how newer information system products can affect the location of where work has to be carried out.
- 'Managing the fact blitz' – shows some of the problems facing accountants when they are faced with increasing amounts of information.
- 'Processing the avalanche: technological tools' – explains some of the IT tools that are available to help manage the information overload that many staff are facing.
- '24-hour global working' – shows how worldwide information systems allow work to be carried out on a worldwide basis.
- 'Lest we forget' – how increased labour mobility may cause retention of information problems for organisations.

4.2 THE EFFECTS OF IT ON WORK PATTERNS

Changes in information technology continue to have effects, not just on methods of information distribution within organisations, but also on the actual work patterns of employees within those organisations. Both of these areas are investigated in the next article.

The distribution of information and effect on work patterns are considered within the same article because one normally affects the other. A few years ago, for example, people may have to had to work close to each other because paper documents had to be shared on a regular basis. If those documents are being transferred electronically then physical location of staff becomes irrelevant. Given the current communications technology, the documents and the information on them can be accessed from London, Leicester or even Lerwick with as much ease as walking across an office to get a piece of paper.

Other examples of technology affecting methods of working in the next article include:

- Maintaining multiple diaries on computer to make joint meetings easier to arrange;
- The transmission of paperless faxes;
- Teleworking and the use of videophones to try to decrease the feeling of isolation that can occur when work is carried out from home.

Although newer technology does remove many of the barriers to the physical location required to perform work, there remains the issue of ensuring that appropriate access can be provided to the information that is needed to carry out work. Although remote access to computer systems is possible, issues such as the cost of telephone lines and the security of data in transit may still need addressing.

JUST PRESS THE BUTTON
Alison Classe, *Softworld Magazine*, 12 January 1995

For anyone selecting a financial IT system, it is vital to consider the purchase in the context of the other systems with which it will interact. That is obvious if the financial systems have to co-exist with other applications, such as manufacturing systems, for instance; less so, perhaps, in the context of office utilities, such as word processors and electronic mail.

But making an office automation system an integral part of any company's systems can allow it to leapfrog its competition through faster dissemination of information.

In the current business climate it is as hard as it has ever been to control administrative costs. Many companies are taking a close look at their administrative processes to find out where bottlenecks and inefficiencies are occurring, with a view to correcting them and so controlling the attendant costs.

The term 'business process re-engineering' is applied freely to this type of activity, although, strictly speaking, BPR denotes a radical approach in which existing organisational structures are broken down and an entire company is reorganised from the ground up, in a way that more closely responds to its customers' needs.

These projects often uncover problems in the way organisations manage their clerical workload.

Besides rationalising clerical processes, applying information technology to what would until recently have been regarded as necessarily manual activities has advantages. In other words, it is now entirely possible to computerise the interstices between the more obvious computer applications.

This is particularly true in the case of organisations that have lots of paper flowing around them, for instance, a building society dealing with mortgage applications.

Documents that get routed through an organisation in a complex way can get lost in someone's in-tray, passed to the wrong person or held up if someone is off ill.

The process often takes longer than necessary. For example, although there is potential for certain parts of the loan application vetting process to take place in parallel, in practice this necessitates photocopying of the document and then marrying up the two copies afterwards, which may be more trouble than it is really worth.

Apart from correcting inherent inefficiencies in the way documents flow around the office, another way of streamlining their passage is to implement 'workflow information systems'. By transferring documents around the office in electronic form, rather than as a piece of paper, staff can reduce the risk of loss and ensure that the paper invariably follows the correct route.

Two people can be working on different aspects of the same document simultaneously. The system can tell managers who is working on any particular document at any moment.

Obviously, to manage workflow electronically, the documents must be converted into an electronic form. That can be done in a variety of ways: by keying in the details from an incoming document; by scanning the document, using an optical scanner that recognises characters and numbers and converts them to a digital form; or by a combination of the two. The original document can then be filed away.

To suit day-to-day conditions, workflow automation systems can make it easy to alter the route that a document takes. For example, if a particular group of workers is understaffed because of illness, it should be easy for a manager to route some of their work to a second group.

Some workflow specialists, such as FileNet, see object-oriented technology as the key to workflow flexibility: using screen graphics that display the process in a diagram, managers can then easily re-channel the flow of work.

What is the relationship between workflow systems and traditional application systems, such as, say, a sales order entry package? The answer should be, 'an intimate one'. Once the information is on the workflow system, it should be possible to put it directly on to relevant application processing systems without rekeying.

So rather than send a sales order that has been taken over the phone to a clerk, who keys it into the sales order entry system, it should be possible for the order, once it has passed the appropriate approval processes, to be automatically entered into the system.

The workflow system will link not only application systems, but also office utilities such as word-processing systems.

Suppose the process of raising a sales order generates a letter – perhaps a letter to the customer to say that his or her credit limit is about to be exceeded. Then, rather than having to pass the order to a secretary, an ordinary PC word processing package can create a standard letter.

In the next few years, the more routine clerical tasks will be done by machines rather than humans, a trend that will either reduce staff levels or allow the same size workforce to handle a much larger and more stimulating workload.

The most important ways in which the clerical and secretarial workload will be reduced can be summarised in one word: integration.

Workflow systems are the most obvious example, but there are many others. Putting someone's diary on to a PC rather than a Filofax may not greatly reduce the effort of looking after it. But once several people's diaries are linked together electronically across a network, there is the potential to schedule meetings at times convenient to all of them, and to let people review, and add provisional appointments to each other's diaries.

Another example of computers taking over the clerical workload is in the management of telephone messages. Messages can be stored on a computer disk as digital voice mail and managed in much the same way as other computer data. It would be nice if the computer could interpret and respond to the message as well, but so far computers are not very good at interpreting the spoken word.

What computers can do, though, is take the 'calling line identification' information from an incoming call and then use that to retrieve data from a computer system.

So, for instance, when a customer phones in with an enquiry about his or her account, the computer can detect the call's originating number as a key to retrieve accounts data from the customer database. So by the time a human operator picks up the call, a screen in front of him or her can already be displaying the customer's account information.

That sort of facility is particularly useful for companies engaged in telemarketing, but it is also relevant to many other situations as well.

Not only do the office systems of the future save effort and improve efficiency, they will also save trees. 'The paperless office' was a catch phrase a few years ago. The slogan seems to have been quietly dropped by the computer industry, possibly because it recognised that computer systems tend to generate miles of paper reports. Nonetheless, offices are gradually moving in a paperless direction.

Even when documents are not being channelled automatically around the office, digitised images can save both paper and space. Digital images on CD-ROM are a more space-efficient way to store reports than on paper. And these images, unlike microfiches, can be recalled from an ordinary computer screen, rather than having to use a special reader.

Then there are paperless faxes. A PC, whether or not part of a network, can generate fax images from computer data without the need to print out a paper report and feed it into a fax machine.

Some application systems have a fax generation capability, so that instead of printing a statement for a customer, he can receive a fax.

If, at the other end, the fax is received not by a fax machine but by another computer, then it can be viewed on screen and need never exist as a physical document.

So instead of a paper document existing in duplicate, as with a traditional fax, it need not exist anywhere except on disk. Like voice messages and other documents, digitised faxes can be stored and organised by computer, thus obviating the need to use filing cabinets.

The logical next step is not to generate a fax image at all, but to transmit the information in the form of characters: electronic mail. E-mail gets a lot of publicity these days, particularly in the context of the Internet, which is the global system of computers connected through the telecommunications network.

For businesses, internal e-mail, delivered virtually instantaneously over a computer network, can be a vastly more efficient and reliable alternative to the conventional internal post system.

Public e-mail systems also facilitate business-to-business communications. Commercial Internet services such as CompuServe can provide secure and reliable e-mail services on the Internet.

However, organisations that have been using e-mail for a while sometimes find that it causes as many problems as it solves.

Pressing a key will send the same message to scores of colleagues, which might seem a good idea at the time but may contribute to a huge electronic rubbish pile that the recipient sees (and probably ignores) the next time they sign on. Junk e-mail is potentially an even more serious problem than ordinary junk mail, because it is so much easier to generate.

The point of e-mail is to share information, and products have come along that take a more rational approach to this task. In particular, Lotus Notes allows groups of colleagues to pool information in a discussion database, rather than send e-mail messages winging in all directions.

Each reader can look at the database and add his or her two-penn'orth to the discussion, secure in the knowledge that the new contribution will be automatically available to all participants. If necessary, multiple copies of the databases can be maintained on different computers on a network. The system maintains them all in line: if a user has a copy of the database on his portable PC, the next time he signs on to the system it will have been brought up to date with any new contributions to the discussions.

Notes, and competing groupware products, are designed to improve the performance of sets of co-workers by optimising the way information is shared. Groupware products are opening up the possibilities for remote working, and for closer co-operation between offices in different locations.

Companies, particularly high technology ones, are realising that they can reduce their office costs vastly by having staff work as far as possible from their own (or customers') premises.

In the past, the main disadvantage of 'teleworking' from the employers' point of view is the danger that teleworking staff would be taken 'out of the information loop'.

Some people doubt whether there is any real substitute for regular face-to-face contact, and most teleworkers do attend team meetings in person.

But with technologies such as videophones and videoconferencing, it is possible to fill any between-meeting gaps as the teleworker confers daily with the supervisor without any need for either one of them to travel.

Workflow systems that link sites across a wide area network will enable tasks to be allocated to remote workers as if they were in the office, and will also allow supervisors to monitor progress.

For remote working to take off, workers clearly need to be given access to the same systems they would have if they were doing their job in the office.

That means that application systems and databases may need to be accessible remotely via a dial-up line (with suitable security being in-built in order to prevent any unauthorised access taking place).

For the small to medium sized company with only a modest administrative burden, the latest office automation developments may on the face of it seem unnecessary.

But the costs of technology are continuing to come down by the minute, unlike the cost of manpower and office space.

Can you be absolutely sure that your office will not be adopting a workflow automation product at some point in the future, or contemplating teleworking in two years' time?

4.3 MANAGING THE FACT BLITZ

One of the main benefits of technological advances over the past ten years or so has been that the quality, and quantity, of information available to accountants has increased significantly. Having more information is not necessarily a bad thing, but when the information being provided exceeds a given amount, then people start finding problems actually using that volume of information.

The term 'human information processor' refers to the idea the people tend to assimilate and process data in much the same way as computers. Data is read from computer screens or books, or heard in meetings or on the telephone. The data has to be stored in the brain and processed in some way so that an individual can use it. There are human problems with using this data, such as only being able to keep a certain number of ideas in current memory at one time, and the time taken to transfer information to long-term memory. This means that all data received may not be utilised simply because it is 'forgotten' or never actually placed in memory due to the large amount of data being received.

The management accountant may be at a particular disadvantage because, not only is the amount of accounting data increasing, but in many organisations the areas of responsibility are also increasing. To use a recent English political phrase, the accountant is hit by a 'double whammy' of information overload, firstly because more information is available from his normal areas of responsibility, but secondly because new information from new responsibility areas must also be assimilated.

To continue to be an effective manager and decision-maker the management accountant will have to develop strategies to cope with the increased volume of information. This can be done in three main ways:

- filtering the information being received so that only the higher-priority or more relevant information is read; or
- investing in some management tools like Expert Systems to help make decisions; or
- delegating responsibility to others.

Unless some action is taken then the quality of decision-making will fall, simply because the management accountant, as an information processor, cannot cope with the large amount of information being given to him. In this article, Diny Slamet investigates the problem of human information processors in more detail, expanding some of the points that have been discussed above. His conclusions concerning how to cope with information overload are realistic, although it would be interesting to see how many accountants actually put them into practice.

MANAGING THE FACT BLITZ

Diny Slamet, *Australian Accountant*, April 1996

Accountants in all areas of the profession are suffering from the stresses of information overload. But nowhere is it felt more acutely than among senior management accountants in companies large and small.

While senior accountants in large companies may feel themselves pulled in many different directions, in smaller operations management accountants can barely keep their heads above water, according to John Corrigan, the technical support officer of the Management Accounting Centre of Excellence.

'In large companies, the chief financial officer or finance director can afford to have a number of specialists to whom the detailed work and detailed control can be relinquished. In a small company, the senior accountant has to cover the full gamut of issues on their own,' he says.

Diversity of issues

As organisations strive to become leaner, more competitive and globally focused, management accountants are working harder than ever before to come to grips with a greater diversity of issues.

Aside from complying with ever-changing rules on taxation and superannuation, and keeping up with new accounting standards and corporate regulations, management accountants are also having their domain stretched to include such areas as management theory, benchmarking, personnel, quality and environmental concerns.

If accountants are managing people they must also be knowledgeable about industrial laws relating to hiring and firing and about sexual harassment and equality issues – more information to add to their already crowded minds.

Bill Ashton, the chief financial officer of Courtaulds (Australia) Pty Ltd and chairman of the Management Accounting COE, believes management accounting is moving away from such fundamentals as costing and budgeting into aspects of corporate operations that involve non-financial measures.

In human resources accounting, for example, management accountants have to deal with intangible concepts such as employee well-being, which can have a direct impact on absenteeism and staff turnover.

'When you look at human resources and the area of enterprise bargaining – which is based on productivity improvements – who's going to tell where the productivity improvements come from, or whether the improvements match the money we pay to employees?' says Ashton.

'Governments are now issuing a proliferation of guidelines and standards on the environment. If a management team wants to target the environment as being important, it's management accountants who have to be able to provide measures and build them into some sort of reporting system.'

Greater management demands

John Corrigan takes the view that many accountants may not be comfortable with the shift away from the traditional accounting role to the greater management role they are increasingly expected to play.

'Accountants now have to understand more about general management philosophies and techniques than they did in the past, when their focus was purely on financial techniques,' he says. 'Some of them may find it difficult to come to grips with the shift towards the team approach and individual empowerment, because empowerment means passing power down. Accountants are often used to having a degree of power because they provide the information and decide who gets it and who doesn't. Empowerment changes all that, and that is an added pressure.'

Others, however, see diversity as a positive challenge. Graham Monk, chief financial officer with Novus Petroleum, thinks that some accountants thrive in the fast, agile and non-bureaucratic nature of a smaller organisation, and is excited by the many different functions he has to perform: dealing with legal issues, marketing, financing, borrowing, tax, hedging and financial risk management.

He admits, however, to sometimes being overwhelmed by regulatory demands.

'As a country and as a business community we are overburdening ourselves with administrative tasks,' he says. 'In the past few years we've worked our way through fringe benefit tax changes, superannuation changes, the industrial relations legislation, the ability to hire and fire, the Companies Code. Superannuation alone changes every year. These kinds of requirements are changing day in and day out.'

Outside help

To make time for strategic thinking, Monk brings in experts to help with tax, superannuation and legal matters.

'You can't be an expert in every area,' he says. 'But you need to keep a finger on it. I believe my responsibility is to know enough about them that you can recognise when you need to call in the experts.'

Corrigan agrees that the trend towards hiring outside expertise will continue to grow, particularly with large companies. According to an informal survey Corrigan conducted of leading chief financial officers, many believe most facets of processing and regulatory reporting will be outsourced to professional firms or specialist contractors in the future. Most external reporting will also be outsourced, allowing finance staff to focus on management reporting.

'Smaller companies, will have a real problem because even now the management accountant is struggling to cope. A potential growth area is that smaller companies will also outsource their entire financial function. They may form networks with other small companies to hire specialist accountants. Otherwise, outsourcing is going to be expensive.'

Graham Monk believes technology holds the key to making life much easier for accountants and is convinced the profession has not applied it in the best possible way.

'As a profession, we've still got a long way to go in using technology. We've used computers to do accounting for the past 30 years, but we're still a very paper-oriented profession. We still have invoices flying around everywhere, we're still producing cheques in great droves, we're still producing paper reports,' he says.

John Corrigan, however, remains unconvinced. 'Some accountants focus too much on technical aspects and forget about the business – and I've seen businesses go under because of that. They focus too much on the process, on getting the numbers, on doing all the models, the what-ifs. I've seen accountants literally sit at a terminal for eight hours a day. You can't get to know a business sitting in front of a computer screen,' says Corrigan.

Generalists or specialists?

While management accountants may have to become generalists who straddle many different functions, accountants on the whole cannot realistically be expected to be experts in every facet of finance.

Bill Ashton predicts that accountants may have to continue their education into areas of specialisation, in much the same way that doctors become specialists.

John Corrigan agrees that the emphasis will be on specialised knowledge and skills, and says accountants will face the added burden of being expected to continue their education throughout their professional lives. No longer will undergraduate qualifications suffice, he says. Corrigan also warns that if the profession becomes too fragmented and specialised, accountants may be hindered from rising through management ranks by their very specialisation.

But Graham Monk disagrees and believes the way the profession is evolving can only bring enormous opportunities for accountants. 'Accountants need to be arming themselves with the skills to take advantage of these opportunities,' says Monk. 'They need to be constantly adding value, analysing, interpreting and making things happen.'

4.4 PROCESSING THE AVALANCHE: TECHNOLOGICAL TOOLS

Many articles in this publication have referred to the problem of information overload, which results from the increasing volumes of information being made available by computer systems. It therefore seems appropriate to consider what technological solutions are currently available now, and may be available in the future, to try to help accountants cope with information overload.

As you would expect, tools to cope with the information overload are running slightly behind those that create the information in the first place, but even so some benefit can be gained now from using them. The three main categories of technological tools currently available are:

- *Search engines* – which perform searches on given text strings within documents to locate information. For example, the word string 'mail merge' could be searched for in a word processing help system. More complicated search engines are available on the Internet, which will search the entire contents of documents on the Web and retrieve those matching the search criteria. Web browsers such as Yahoo and Alta Vista fall into this category.
- *Information filters* – which have the opposite job of search engines, that is, they only allow certain information to be displayed. In other words, information that does not meet certain pre-set criteria is not brought to the manager's attention.
- *Information agents* – are a newer development with limited use as yet. An information agent is a computer search program that the user instructs with preferences of the information to be received. For example, the user may need information on weather conditions in Mexico, or the coffee crop in Brazil. The agent will then be sent out into the Internet or similar system to find this information. It will report back to the user when information meeting the desired criteria has been found. Although agents are similar to search engines, they contain much more complex programming and have the ability to judge whether an article is relevant and even make copies of themselves should the volume of information become too large to handle.

The next article by David Neiger explains the first two tools in some detail. Information agents are still relatively new, although good computer magazines will normally provide examples of them.

PROCESSING THE AVALANCHE: TECHNOLOGICAL TOOLS

David Neiger, *Australian Accountant*, April 1996

Like it or not, the information age is upon us. Never before has it been so easy to communicate with people irrespective of distance, time zones and political barriers. With the convergence of telecommunications and computer technology it is no more difficult or expensive to send a message to the United States or Russia than it is to send a message around the corner.

While this technology enables vast quantities of information to be created and disseminated, the tools and technology to sort and filter this information are still primitive. As a result people begin to feel overwhelmed by the incredible amounts of information available and as a result start to suffer from what is commonly called 'information overload'.

In the absence of suitable tools to assist with the processing. managers and employees are forced to spend their time manually processing information rather than utilising knowledge to assist with wealth creation. As a result, the information age is actually adding to the cost of business rather than reducing it.

It will be some time before it is possible to purchase an effective search engine or 'information processor' off the shelf and load it as one would load a word processor or spreadsheet. Currently the only tools available are simple search engines (computer programs which have been designed to locate information), information filters (which are programs designed to sort and prioritise information) and information agents.

Even though these tools lack basic intelligence and common sense, they are still much better than not having anything at all — or worse, being totally starved of information.

Search engines

Most available search engines can be found as add-ons to other tools such as word processors, databases, spreadsheets, CD ROM references and operating systems (such as Fast Find in Windows 95 and grep in Unix).

These search engines sift through available information and locate words or phrases which exactly match the information requested (the search criterion or the query). This is useful if you only want to find a particular word or phrase in a document but is of limited use if you are trying to locate documents relating to a topic or concept.

In practice, the majority of queries are vague or ambiguous and as a result the search engines either fail to find the information or find too much information.

Even the more complex search engines available on the Internet (such as Alto Vista, Yahoo or NetSearch) are not much better. A good example of this is when you use one of these search engines to locate Web sites. For instance, if you are looking for sites which contain information on tax, you will most probably find hundreds of sites (or, in computer jargon, score hundreds of hits). Most probably you will find that you have been given so much information that you are still unable to locate the relevant Web site or you spend so much time sifting through sites that you would have been better off calling the tax office directly.

If you narrow down your search too much, you also risk failing to find information. For example, if you search the Web for information on 'tax avoidance', you may not locate sites which have strategies for 'tax minimisation' or 'family trusts' simply because the search engine is unable to realise that these concepts are related.

Another problem is that in the absence of 'artificial intelligence', computers determine 'relevance' by the number of times a particular word or phrase appears. This generally leads to absurd results whereby a site which contains a poorly written protest about tax will be ranked higher than the Australian Tax Office site simply because the protest site contains the word 'tax' hundreds of time whereas the ATO site only contains ten instances of the word.

Information filters

While search engines are used to locate information, information filters are used for exactly the opposite: that is, they are used to reduce the information torrent into a more manageable flow.

The prime function of an information filter is to sort through the hundreds of electronic mail messages (e-mails) and millions of news articles (which are transmitted on Usenet news and AAP news feeds) to determine which articles are relevant and should be passed through the filter, and which items are irrelevant and should either be assigned a lower priority or discarded.

According to Professor Andrew Jenlings of RMIT in Melbourne, the main problem with these types of systems is that they fail to take into account a user's changing needs and requirements. He compares these systems to a substitute secretary who will obediently pass on calls which satisfy a certain criteria (for example, internal calls from management), take messages from other callers (spouse, colleagues and certain named clients) and discard all other calls.

The problem both with the substitute secretary and the information filters is that they cannot deal with situations which have not been explicitly explained or which have changed. For example, if Bob (who is the CEO) rings from an unusual number and merely identifies himself as Bob, the substitute secretary would be unable to recognise him. As a result, the substitute secretary – like an information filter – would fail to pass on the message.

According to Dr John Shepherd of the University of NSW, in addition to this type of information filter, there are also adaptive filters which can 'learn' the user's requirements and continuously refine the filter.

These adaptive filters work in two ways. One type requires explicit feedback from the users. It asks the user to rank or rate the article and to classify whether the article is relevant or irrelevant. It then uses this information to update the rule base and further refine the filter. As a result, the filter may become too effective and filter out articles which the user actually wanted to read. This leads to a situation where the user is unaware that the required articles exist and as a result does not know that they are missing out on information.

The other type of adaptive filter works on implicit feedback from the users. It monitors the user and attempts to glean the knowledge from their behaviour. For example, if a user discards all articles with certain words in the title, the system assumes that the user is not interested in articles containing those specific (or related) words and accordingly filters out those articles in future.

However, the systems are unable to distinguish between certain types of behaviour. For example, if a user started reading an article but was distracted by a telephone call, the system would assume that the user was very interested in that type of article (because they spent 20 minutes reading it) and would accordingly permit all articles relating to similar topics even though the user, in reality, hated the article and was just about to delete it.

In other words, the system will do its best, but sometimes its best is far from good. Its shortcomings serve to underline the point that no matter how sophisticated and accurate these systems claim to be, they are no substitute for common sense and diligence.

4.5 24-HOUR GLOBAL WORKING

Articles in this section have been investigating the effect of technology and changing information systems on employment and on our ability to use the information that is being made available. One area that has not yet been investigated is the overall effect on working patterns of the ability to transfer information around the world quickly and efficiently. With many international organisations being linked by their own data networks, there are few, if any, barriers to transferring information from any location to another location, anywhere in the world. This does give rise to queries concerning the security of that data in transit, but the focus here is on how this data transfer affects the overall working environment.

Given that information can be transferred easily, there is no reason for teams of people who are working on the same project to be located in the same city, or even the same country. There are obviously inter-personnel issues to address if individuals do not meet each other, but if global information sharing works, then significant increases in productivity can be achieved. To take a simple example, I could send this article to a colleague in, say, Phoenix, Arizona, at 5.30 p.m. (I am based in the UK) when I finish work. My colleague will receive the article mid-morning in Phoenix, when it could be proofread while I am having my supper. The article can then be e-mailed back to me so that, first thing in the morning, I can check the amendments, action these and send the completed script to the publisher. Sending the article to a colleague in a different time zone has effectively saved a day in the editorial process. This may not appear to be a large improvement, but as examples in the next article show, multiplying this principle over the life of a project will provide significant time savings.

A similar system could be used in many other situations, for example to prepare information for important meetings. Why not send European company statistics to New York, where US information can be added, then on to Tokyo for the Far East summary, and then back to Europe for an important board meeting? This would ensure that up-to-date information is added to the board agenda and avoid a rush of preparing the information in Europe just before the meeting commences.

Information-sharing on a global basis may have significant benefits for software development, as the article shows, although the principle could be applied to many other situations. It is a useful alternative to consider when development or processing time is critical.

24-HOUR GLOBAL WORKING

***Business Computer World*, July/August 1997**

On first hearing, it sounds like a daft idea. A team of programmers in Europe works on a project during the day. At clocking-off time, it sends the work to another team in North America, which continues development during its day. Eight hours later, the work moves on to Asia, where another shift takes over. Finally, it arrives back in Europe, ready for the cycle to be repeated.

Surprisingly, this idea not only works, it is bringing substantial benefits to those who practise it Several large companies – and a few smaller ones – have found that 24-hour global working is a practical way of accelerating software development. Its use isn't limited to computing; engineers and architects, among others, are finding ways of exploiting it.

Of course, not all development work lends itself to this approach. For it to succeed, you need a project that can easily be broken down into small units, with a well-defined interface between tasks.

One example involves programmers in Asia designing and coding small, self-contained components. At the end of the working day, these components are passed to a quality assurance team in the US. By the time the Asian programmers arrive back at work the next morning, their code has been tested and the bug reports are waiting on their desks. The result: elapsed time for the project is cut by half.

This is precisely what IBM is doing to develop Javabeans components for its Visual Age environment. The components are being developed by teams at Tsinghua University in China, the Belarus Institute of Computer Science and the Tata Group in India. Another team, in Seattle, is responsible for integration, quality assurance and usability testing. By moving the work around the globe every 24 hours, each iteration of the code/test cycle takes one day rather than two to three.

But cutting development time is not the only advantage. All the companies we spoke to cited availability of skills as a significant reason for adopting the technique. While Europe and North America are suffering a shortage of development staff, Asian countries – especially India and China – have plenty of experienced programmers, many of them with skills that are hard to find in the West.

So how does it work in practice? The system clearly requires fast and reliable communication links. It also needs a sophisticated version control regime that obliges team members to check work into and out of a central repository. This ensures everyone is working on the latest version and one programmer's work will never overwrite another's.

IBM is using Teamconnection as a version control system, with Lotus Domino as a collaboration server. Other companies are using equally sophisticated tools. In the case of small projects, simple e-mail and file transfer systems might be adequate. With communications costs falling, the expense of these systems is rarely a factor.

Until now, 24-hour working has been mainly confined to software development projects. But users in other disciplines are also discovering its benefits. At civil engineering company Ove Arup, it is crucial to a large construction project. And several architectural firms are using it to speed up the production of routine drawings.

In one sense, there is nothing novel in this. Professional staff are accustomed to collaborating over long distances, often without ever meeting their co-workers face to face. What's new is the way in which these people are treating time zones: not as an obstacle to communication; rather, as a way of squeezing three shifts into one.

Subject: James Martin & Co.
Projects: year 2000 conversions and other software development

Last year, James Martin & Co., one of the world's leading software houses, joined forces with the giant HCL Corporation of New Delhi. The combined group boasts 3,200 software professionals in 57 offices throughout Europe, the US, India and the Pacific Rim. Its mission: to offer specialist help with large-scale software maintenance projects. For the next two years it expects to have its hands full with year 2000 conversions.

The use of 24-hour global development is a vital part of the company's methods. 'It means we can increase the speed of delivery, enjoy more intimate client involvement and have more skills brought to bear on the project,' says Stephen Izatt, chief operating officer of James Martin & Co., Europe. We are primarily working with global customers, so we can facilitate their own 24-hour working through our teams.'

Most of the company's year 2000 projects are handled at development centres in India and the Philippines, while the project management is carried out at locations convenient for the clients. This succeeds, according to Izatt, because all the staff are trained in the same rigorous development processes. 'This has facilitated a fairly unique way of developing in an iterative lifecycle, despite the geographical split,' he explains.

One reason why India and the Philippines were chosen for the centres was the use of English as a main language in those countries. This has eliminated one of the more common difficulties of global working. However, cultural differences cause occasional problems. 'We are learning about these all the time,' says Izatt

With its vast army of programmers, the company can call on a wide variety of specialist skills. But to take advantage of global working, it has found it necessary to concentrate on specific development languages and platforms. Most of its current work is concentrated on Oracle, DB2, Powerbuilder, Composer, Entera and Redbrick.

Communication between the centres is carried out by high-capacity frame relays, using a custom-built intranet. Routine contacts are handled by linked Meridian voice-mail and e-mail systems, while Intel Proshare is used for video-conferencing. Another important component is the Architect system, which James Martin produces itself. The company describes this as a tool for process management, this being a super-set of project management.

'Architect's workflow management uses e-mail to distribute tasks, prerequisites, process guidance and metrics to a scattered workforce,' says Izatt. 'A central repository then captures the actuals on completed work and keeps project management completely informed on progress. It also uses captured metrics to help improve estimating.'

He says 24-hour global working is expensive to set up, but most of the company's initial investment was recouped in the first two years. The running costs are also high, although they are decreasing as the price of the technology comes down.

'Not all projects will be suitable for this approach, but many are,' says Izatt. 'It has established itself in our global practice. As communications technology becomes cheaper, easier to use and more powerful, we are seeing an increase in this way of working. It is now part of our capability and our culture.'

Subject: Ove Arup
Project: Bangkok Elevated Road and Train System (Berts)

Thailand is, in parts, a beautiful country. But its capital, Bangkok, is a noisy, polluted city with traffic congestion that would be inconceivable even in London or Los Angeles. To solve the city's problems, Hong Kong-based Hopewell Holdings was awarded a contract to build and operate an ambitious integrated transport system. Known as Berts, it includes an elevated main-line railway, high-capacity metro and three-lane toll expressway.

The size, complexity and tight timescales of the Berts project has led to the adoption of some innovative working practices. The detailed design is being carried out by civil engineering company Ove Arup. It has about 70 professional staff assigned to the project, based in London. The company also has a project office in Hong Kong which liaises with the client on detailed design issues. Also in Hong Kong, a geotechnics team monitors site investigations and provides guidelines for pile design.

Drawings, reports and detailed calculations are produced in London, in response to design requests from Hong Kong. The work is carried out in Intergraph and Autocad, and is transmitted by a dedicated ISDN line leased from Cable & Wireless. The Intergraph system maintains a three-dimensional digital survey of the system's route. The Autocad system produces layered structural and services drawings, which are sent to Hong Kong as plot files.

As far as the engineers in Hong Kong are concerned, this is an overnight service. Because of the eight-hour time difference, staff in the East can request design changes in the evening and have the updated drawings on their screens the next day.

As the design details are received in Hong Kong, they are assembled into design submission packages which are forwarded by satellite link to Bangkok. There, a quality assurance team is overseeing the work and liaising with the Thai transport authorities.

But wouldn't it have been more efficient to base the entire project under one roof in

Bangkok? 'Yes, but it would also have been more expensive and disruptive,' says Duncan Wilkinson, associate director of Ove Arup.

'The project requires about 150 engineers, specialists and technicians, with skills that are not readily available in Thailand. We have the skills, but not in one place. With modern communications, it is easier to mobilise people in their own offices than to move them to the other side of the world.'

However, Wilkinson does admit that the lack of personal contact between team members has sometimes proved a problem. The fact that there is only a small overlap in the working day restricts telephone contact, although it does not affect fax or e-mail. But Wilkinson is convinced that these disadvantages are easily offset by the benefits of 24-hour working. Without it, it would have been impossible to meet the project's demanding timescale.

'The ability to work a 24-hour day has been a positive advantage,' says Wilkinson. 'We will do it again on other projects, especially when distant markets open up in areas where we don't currently have an office. Berts certainly isn't a one-off.'

24-Hour global working lessons:

1. Establish a common working language for the project. As far as possible, recruit your teams in countries where this language is widely spoken.
2. Be sensitive to cultural differences. Take advice on these and educate your staff accordingly.
3. Install the best possible communications infrastructure and include plenty of spare capacity. The cost will be small compared with the benefits of the project.

4.6 LEST WE FORGET

One of the main trends in employment in recent years has been employees spending less time in each job before moving on to their next challenge in another organisation. This trend has resulted partly from companies themselves employing staff on short-term contracts and partly from many employees making a greater number of strategic career changes to enhance their CVs.

The trend in decreasing the number of full-time longer-serving employees may result in some benefits to organisations like decreased overhead and redundancy costs, but it has a worrying trend for continuity within an organisation. Almost all employees will accumulate specialist information concerning the organisation that they are working for during their time of employment there. If an employee leaves then that information and associated experience goes with them. The employee will have benefited from the accumulated knowledge and can use it in their next job. However, the information and experience is lost from the organisation. The issue addressed in this article is how to keep that knowledge and experience within the organisation while allowing for increased labour flexibility.

You will find that part of the solution to retaining knowledge in the organisation is enhancing the exit interview process for employees. However, a longer-term solution will need some form of library being established to keep the important information available within the organisation for an appropriate amount of time.

LEST WE FORGET

Anita van de Vliet, *Management Today*, January 1997

Have you found yourself grumbling recently at yet another request for contributions to a gift for yet another departing employee? Your company should see more serious cause for concern. For these departing individuals will take with them not just their farewell tokens, but all the knowledge and experience they have gathered through their years at the company.

This complex knowledge might include the individual's experience of particular events and projects, lists of clients and contacts, and an awareness of decision-making styles and company culture. It will also include assumptions (often unspoken) about the firm's informal working practices and relationships, what 3M calls the 'shadow organisation' or grapevine that communicates 'how things really get better round here'.

Collectively, this knowledge forms what is variously known as organisational or corporate memory, and the body should be regarded as the firm's intellectual capital and a major resource. But most companies in the UK have no way of capturing and recording this knowledge, whether for the purposes of passing it on to newcomers or allowing existing managers to draw on it for instruction. Indeed, they do not see the necessity, believing in the value of change and new brooms sweeping clean rather than in the lessons of history. The fact that business history is a neglected topic in Britain is illustrated by the detail that here there are just three professors in the subject, compared with over 400 in Japan. 'We prefer to look to the future rather than back at the past' is a typical response when you enquire after British company policy.

But while there are obviously dangers in dwelling on the past, there are equal dangers in remaining in ignorance of it. Studies at Warwick University have shown that many companies reproduce their blunders on a regular basis, while management consultants McKinsey have concluded that many waste time and resources resolving problems that have already been unravelled in the company: reinventing the wheel is a 'much more common drain of cash and creativity than most managers imagined'.

The dangers of corporate memory loss are particularly acute in an era when downsizing and re-engineering have shortened job tenure to an average six years, against the backdrop of an eight-year trade cycle, comments Arnold Kransdorff of Pencorp, the London-based business historians. He cites as one example the case of a leading building society which found, at the beginning of the 1989/90 housing market collapse, that it no longer had any senior managers at branch level who could remember first-hand how the organisation had handled the previous housing market downturn. Ironically, he points out, now that the housing market is recovering, there are apparently once again 'few managers who can remember how the organisation responded to the last upturn'.

Corporate amnesia can also be the result of the trend towards outsourcing, according to Margaret Graham, founding partner of the Winthrop Group in Cambridge, Massachusetts, one of the leading corporate memory and business history consultants in the US. Companies intent on reducing their capital base or hiving off a problem by outsourcing a function forget the importance of 'local knowledge, specific to the company', with serious consequences for productivity. 'An awareness of history can play an important role at all times of change – re-engineering, growth initiatives, selecting a new leader, launching new products, mergers and acquisitions,' she adds.

So how do you go about capturing and recording the company's collective knowledge? One obvious method is the exit interview – not the traditional, formulaic twenty questions routinely posed in many companies, but a carefully structured and well-researched debriefing, based on a knowledge of the individual's career and expertise. 'Every individual and every job is different,' points out Kransdorff, 'so you can't just use a carbon copy format.' The interview is geared to extracting the detail of events and projects, a flotation, perhaps, or product design or marketing strategy, and to capturing the nuances of the company culture. In both the UK and the US, this sort of detailed debriefing still tends to be reserved for senior managers, although studies are now showing the importance here of supervisors and middle managers, so the net may widen (certainly, the Japanese believe in the value of supervisors and middle managers as keepers of the corporate memory).

In Kransdorff's experience, exit interviews last on average half a day (with a break to draw breath in the middle), although somebody with 15 years' experience to impart may need several sessions. Speaking is better than writing, simply because most managers are better at the former, he says. And as Elizabeth Adkins, archives manager at Kraft Foods in the US, points out, 'Retirement is a good time to talk: the history is still recent enough to recall, and people are ready to relax a little, to talk about the issues'. At Kraft, the interview will be preserved in transcript, edited only for hesitations and lapses of grammar, and can be used to speed up the process of induction, plugging the newcomer into the company scene. It will also be indexed, stored in an archival database, complete with index and abstract, and ready for future reference. 'This way, individuals are still able to be of value, even after they have left the company,' says Kransdorff.

Another way of building up oral history is to interview key individuals during their actual employment, thus avoiding the dangers of the distortions of memory – the glamorising, glossing over, or simply forgetting. These interviews can take place either at regular intervals of every nine or 12 months, suggests Kransdorff, or at the conclusion of important projects.

Or it can be useful to track important corporate projects while they are unfolding. The Pencorp approach is to debrief decision-makers in the equivalent of an oral diary: at the end of the project, a suitably edited transcript contains unequivocal, sequential evidence of how and why individuals made their decisions at the time. This is subjected to the scrutiny of independent functional experts, who also produce a learning audit for the company that specifically identifies lessons which can be applied in the future.

The learning audit is a development of the post-implementation review, such as the three-year Project Homework carried out by senior employees at Boeing before the development of its 757 and 767 aircraft. This studied the managerial failures and successes of past development processes and then came up with hundreds of recommendations, after which several members of the team transferred to the 757 and 767 start-up projects: the result was the most problem-free product launch in Boeing's history. Business historians would argue that tracking the project while it is in progress has the further advantage of showing the actual circumstances in which decisions were made.

The corporate history in book form can also be useful, if used not as whitewash but as learning tool, as can a detailed product history. Corporate memory consultants stress the value too of professionally managed archives – a sadly neglected sphere in the UK. Managing an archive so that it can be fruitfully used involves more than simply collecting items, explains Graham. 'Live interviews, for example, should be made accessible both topically and interpretatively,' she advises. They should be annotated by subject, and illuminated with a short history and comment to provide the context.

Increasingly, the best-managed archives are incorporating what the Fuji-Xerox company calls 'registered know-how', that is, the knowledge which is really critical to the company. And the most advanced corporations are now building their archives into their intranets. For a good example of the latest advances, look no further than management consultants Booz-Allen & Hamilton and their 'knowledge programme'.

The programme was developed some two and a half years ago, explains Jan Torsilieri, principal and member of the original 'core knowledge team', and has since been introduced to a wide range of clients who, like Booz-Allen itself, have identified knowledge as a key component. Incorporated in a third-generation intranet network, the programme now contains some 3,000 documents, and is constantly being augmented. Knowledge creation comes not only from the firm's global innovation teams (composed of senior staff, seconded for two years at a time and charged with developing the firm's intellectual capital) but from all staff, at all levels: at the end of each client engagement, any 'frameworks' or generic lessons that have emerged are fed into the programme. The information is accessible to all, but at different levels, depending on the employee's status in the company.

The programme is headed by a 'chief knowledge officer' and managed by some twelve to fifteen knowledge managers or super-librarians, as she describes them, who combine expertise in library science with an understanding of the consulting world, supported by some 85 researchers. The knowledge managers are an integral part of the consultancy staff, working with the partners when launching client engagements, and coming up with suggestions: their understanding of what is in effect the firm's corporate memory means they have a very good overview.

Any such intranet-based knowledge programme implies a culture shift towards greater openness, a considerable challenge. But the merit of such a move also needs to be accurately measured, which is probably the hardest part of all, says Torsilieri. 'We are absolutely convinced of its value,' she says, but while both profits and turnover have increased dramatically since the system's introduction, it is of course difficult to prove cause and effect. The benefits of the programme do seem to have registered on other more precise measures, however: 'We've published more books, and we're being quoted more in other publications. We are also continuing to commit our senior players to the programme, which reflects the belief that it's worth it.'

In the case of management consultants, it may seem self-evident that the firm's collective knowledge is its most valuable resource. Kraft Foods provides an example of the value of well-managed archives in a very different industry. With material dating back to 1780 (when the company's first product, Bakers Chocolate, came out), the Kraft archives have been professionally managed since 1984. The call for such management came from a number of quarters, explains Adkins, including the company's PR and legal departments, its advertising department, staff engaged in strategic reviews of product planning, and the marketing people trying to get the most out of the equity invested in the Kraft trademark. The number of different audiences interested has helped the system succeed, she believes.

The archives now contain some 6,000 cubic feet of documentary records: biographical files, minutes of meetings, legal and research documents, advertising, marketing files, and oral history, consisting of transcribed interviews with all employees on their retirement. These interviews are conducted by archives staff, and the results 'personify our corporate memory, and give us a deeper understanding of company history,' says Adkins. 'We research each career and the kind of events people experienced, and prepare questions on the relevant subjects.'

Perhaps the most obvious use of the Kraft archives is in marketing and advertising campaigns, which can draw on a particular product's heritage. A successful relaunch of Cracker Barrel cheese, for example, was based partly on how the product was sold in the 1960s, when sales began to take off; and 'Interactive Kitchen', the company's Internet home page, draws on the Kraft tradition as part of the American way, on its leadership in creative kitchens, and on its pioneering approach to adopting new media.

The archives department is also involved in strategic reviews, says Adkins, such as the recent taskforce study on the advantages of growth by acquisition compared with growth through product development. This conducted an 'assessment of the company's record over the last 25 years, of what worked, and what didn't', she says.

Broadly speaking, Adkins adds, corporate history is useful as a source of 'feelings of continuity, particularly at a time of change'. It can be reassuring, she suggests, for employees currently involved in a merger to know that this is not the first time former competitors have been expected to work together: the 1920s and 1930s were in this way very similar to the 1980s and 1990s.